AVRO
VULCAN

1952 onwards (B2 model)

COVER CUTAWAY: **Avro Vulcan B2.** *Mike Badrocke*

Tony Blackman, Andrew Edmondson and Alfred Price
have asserted their moral rights to be identified as the
authors of this work.

First published in June 2010
Reprinted in September 2010 and January 2011

A catalogue record for this book is available from the
British Library

ISBN 978 1 84425 831 4

Library of Congress control no. 2010921624

Published by Haynes Publishing,
Sparkford, Yeovil, Somerset BA22 7JJ, UK
Tel: 01963 442030 Fax: 01963 440001
Int. tel: +44 1963 442030 Int. fax: +44 1963 440001
E-mail: sales@haynes.co.uk
Website: www.haynes.co.uk

Haynes North America Inc.
861 Lawrence Drive, Newbury Park,
California 91320, USA

Printed in the USA by Odcombe Press LP,
1299 Bridgestone Parkway, La Vergne, TN 37086

Acknowledgements

The authors wish to place on record the invaluable
assistance received from the following individuals
during the preparation of this book: Dr Robert Pleming,
'Jeff' Jefford, Mike Pearson, Tony Regan, Peter West,
Martin Withers, Peter Thomas and Alan Baxter. To
all these gentlemen, the authors tender their grateful
thanks.

Unless otherwise stated, all images and drawings
reproduced in this book are the copyright of The Vulcan
to the Sky Trust (www.vulcantothesky.org). The authors
would also like to thank the following institutions and
individuals who have supplied information and images
for use in this book: the Avro Heritage Trust; the
Imperial War Museum, London; Phil Whalley of the
Vulcan Restoration Trust (www.avrovulcan.com); Fred
Martin of RZF Digital; Damien Burke; Jonathan Falconer
and Steve Rendle of Haynes Publishing;
JCB; Ian Black; D. Petrie; Ian Waudby; Glen Ambler;
Peter R. March/PRM Aviation; Andy Leitch
(www.avrovulcan.org); and Dave Morris, Chief Engineer
at the Fleet Air Arm Museum, Yeovilton.

AVRO
VULCAN

VULCAN TO THE SKY
HONOURING THE PAST, INSPIRING THE FUTURE

1952 onwards (B2 model)

Owners' Workshop Manual

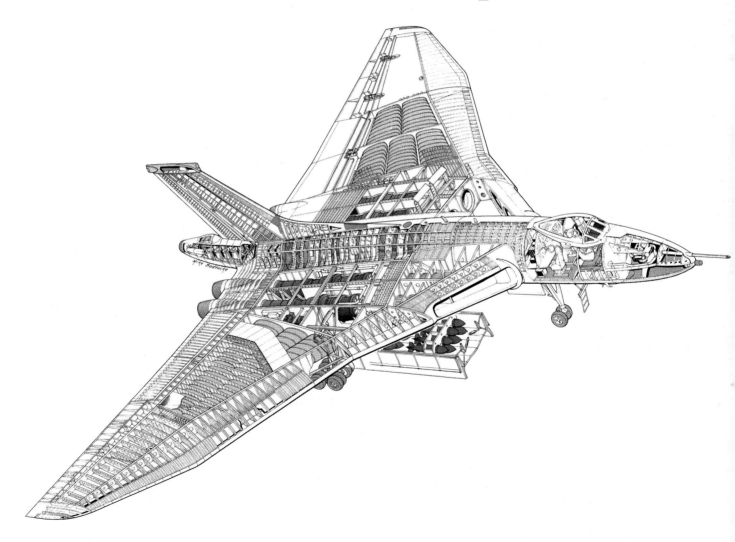

An insight into owning, restoring, servicing and flying
Britain's iconic Cold War bomber

Alfred Price, Tony Blackman and Andrew J. K. Edmondson

Contents

6   The Vulcan Story

The competition	8
Flying scale models	10
Maiden flight	12
The B1 in production	14
Enter the B2	15
The switch to low altitude	23
Improved capability	27
Reconnaissance role	31
Tanker vulcans	32

36   When the Vulcan Went to War

When diplomacy failed	38
'Looks like we've got a job of work, fellers ...'	39
'It was dreadfully turbulent ...'	41
Final preparations for attack	42
'Superfuse!'	44
What did the Vulcan Black Buck missions achieve?	49

50   Anatomy of the Vulcan B2

Airframe	54
Olympus engines	63
Engine starting	67
Electrical system	68
Powered flying controls	69
Air brakes	70
Fuel system	71
Landing gear	73
Airborne Auxiliary Power Plant (AAPP)	75
Bomb bay doors	76
Brake parachute	77
Pneumatic system	77

78   The Pilot's View

Introduction to the Vulcan	80
Learning to fly the Vulcan	88
In the descent and landing	92

96   The Navigator's View

104   The AEO's View

114   The Crew Chief's View

Pre-flight Inspection	116
Refuelling	116
Crew Chief checks	118
Post-flight inspection	120

122   Vulcan to the Sky

Into private hands	124
A chance encounter	125
Amassing support	125
Enter the Heritage Lottery Fund	127
Lottery success	128
Financial problems	129
A massive job	130
First flight post-restoration	130
New financial crisis	133

134   The Restoration of Vulcan XH558

154   Appendices

Appendix A – Avro Vulcan timeline	154
Appendix B – Surviving Vulcans	156
Appendix C – Glossary of terms	157

158   Index

Chapter 1

The Vulcan Story

When the prototype Avro Vulcan made its first appearance in public at the 1952 Farnborough Air Show, it stole the limelight. With its highly swept delta wing and tailless configuration, the new bomber looked every inch a world-beater. Compared with the Avro Lancaster, its predecessor of a decade earlier, in its production version the new bomber would fly more than twice as fast, more than twice as high and more than twice as far.

OPPOSITE Avro Vulcans of 617 Squadron (in the foreground) in their anti-flash white nuclear bomber paint scheme line-up at RAF Scampton in 1963. Behind them are six Handley Page Victor B2 aircraft. *IWM RAF T5321*

The Vulcan story had its origins in 1946, when the British government launched a secret programme to design, build and test a nuclear weapon. At that time it was believed that only by the possession of such a weapon, could the nation retain its role as a major player on the world stage.

Possession of the devastating new weapon would count for little, however, unless the nation also possessed a viable means to deliver it. To that end, in December 1946, the Ministry of Supply issued Specification B35/46 calling for a high-performance long-range bomber able to carry a nuclear weapon. The requirement specified a jet propelled aircraft with a maximum speed of 500kts, an over-target altitude of 50,000ft and a range of 3,350 nautical miles. The aircraft was to be able to carry a single nuclear weapon 25ft long, 5ft wide and weighing up to 10,000lbs, or a similar weight of high-explosive bombs. It was hoped to bring the new bomber into service in 1951.

The new breed of bomber would deliver its attack at speeds within one decimal place of the speed of sound. Back in 1946, it seemed that such a performance would render these aircraft almost invulnerable to fighter attack. The reason for this confidence was the phenomenon of compressibility or, as it became popularly known at the time, 'The Sound Barrier'. The effects of compressibility varied from aircraft to aircraft, but at that time it seemed that the immutable laws of physics imposed a maximum speed at which an aircraft could be controlled. Any fighter trying to engage a bomber flying at nine-tenths the speed of sound, Mach .93, would need to have a margin of overtaking speed but that would take it very close to the speed of sound. As a fighter advanced past its compressibility threshold, shock waves upset the airflow over the aircraft and caused the controls to lose their effect. At best the phenomenon might prevent accurate gunnery. At worst the fighter might enter an uncontrolled dive, from which the pilot regained control at too low an altitude to be able to pull out. Nobody would do that twice.

In the years to follow it would become clear that the so-called sound barrier did not exist, and that with careful design and sufficient engine power a fighter could exceed the speed of sound safely. Nevertheless, the new type of bomber would still pose a severe threat to any current or foreseen air defence system.

The competition

In the lean years immediately after the Second World War, B35/46 was by far the largest development programme in prospect for Britain's struggling aircraft companies. Six firms tendered bids to meet the requirement of which two, Armstrong Whitworth and English Electric, were soon eliminated from the competition. The four remaining firms, Short Brothers, Vickers, Handley Page and Avro all produced credible proposals for the design of four-engined jet bombers.

The straight winged Short SA-4, (later named the Sperrin) was technically the least advanced of the designs but it was also the least risky. Although it would not meet the B35/46 requirement in several respects, it would serve as a low risk 'back-stop' for the new bomber programme.

BELOW Centre of attention: the prototype Vulcan, VX770, pictured during its public debut at the Farnborough Air Show in September 1952.
Avro Heritage Trust (AHT)

Next in order of complexity was the Vickers 660 (later named the Valiant). This aircraft had a moderately swept wing and it too would not meet the requirements of OR229 in full. Nevertheless, it was closer to that goal than the SA-4. The Air Ministry regarded the Vickers entry as a further intermediate solution, while it awaited the success or otherwise of the two most advanced designs.

The Handley Page HP 80 (later named the Victor), was a full blooded attempt to meet the B35/46 requirement. It featured the so-called 'crescent wing', with a high degree of sweep back at the wing roots, blending into moderate sweep back at the wing tips.

Finally there was the Avro submission, the delta-winged Avro 698 (later named the Vulcan), another full-blooded attempt at the B35/46 requirement. The company's chief designer at that time, Roy Chadwick, had also led the team that designed the highly successful Lancaster bomber. Chadwick decided the best way to meet the specification was to employ a large delta wing without a tail plane, with the fuselage buried in the wing roots. The attractions of that layout were:

■ The pronounced sweep-back of the wing leading edge would delay the onset of buffet

and drag on the top surface of the wing, when flying at high sub-sonic speeds.
■ The delta wing could have a large area without the need for a large span.
■ The delta wing would have two spars, one at the leading edge and one at the trailing edge, meeting at the wing tip, instead of a conventional single main spar. That meant that the wing could have a very stiff structure.
■ A delta wing would have a very long chord at the wing root, and it would be very thick. That thickness would provide room to bury the engine air intakes, the engines themselves, and for the undercarriage when it was retracted. In addition, a thick wing would provide room in which to bury the fuel tanks.

The Air Ministry liked the Avro and the Handley Page submissions, and selected both for further development. When the delta wing was chosen for the Avro 698 there was little background experience on how it would perform in flight. It is possible that Avro received help from the Royal Aircraft Establishment (RAE) at Farnborough, which would have received data from wind tunnel studies carried out in Germany during the Second World War.

ABOVE The formidable trio: a formation of the three RAF Mark 1 V-bombers with the Vulcan in the lead, followed by a Valiant and a Victor. These three early production aircraft were undergoing tests at A&AEE Boscombe Down in 1957.

Unfortunately for the project Roy Chadwick was killed in 1947, when the Avro Tudor airliner in which he was flying crashed during a test flight. The loss of this talented and much respected designer had an immediate impact on the company's proposal for the new bomber. The Air Ministry decided to delay authorisation to begin construction of the Avro 698, until it was convinced that Avro possessed the design competence needed to handle such an advanced design.

Vickers received instructions to proceed with the construction of two Type 660 prototypes in April 1948. In the same month, Handley Page was contracted to produce two HP80 prototypes and Short Brothers followed with an order for two SA-4 prototypes later in the year.

Stuart Davies took over as Chief Designer at Avro and in June 1948 the company finally received an order to construct two Type 698 prototypes. At the time it was believed that the RAF would place a large order for only one of the new B.35/46 bomber designs. That led to a period of intensive rivalry between Avro and the other three aircraft companies, and latterly between Avro and Handley Page.

One can speculate on the extent to which the new Avro bomber would have turned out differently, had Roy Chadwick still been in charge of the project. Certainly a decision was taken later, to place the fuselage between the two wing roots rather than have it buried in them. That made it easier to fit in the pressurised cabin for the crew and other necessary items of equipment.

Flying scale models

It was one thing to draw up plans for an aircraft with a futuristic looking shape, it was quite another to produce a shape that would fly without unpleasant, perhaps dangerous, handling characteristics. To allay these concerns it was decided to construct a small number of one-third scale flying models of the Type 698, designated Avro 707s, to test various aspects of the handling of the full sized aircraft. Among the issues needing to be resolved were:

- Would the elevators on the trailing edge of the wing give sufficient control authority without a separate tail plane?
- Would there be sufficient damping in pitch?
- Would the fin and rudder alone provide sufficient directional stability?
- Would the rudder cope with the different asymmetric power with two engines shut down?
- Would the stalling behaviour be benign? In particular would it avoid the nasty stalling characteristics – like pitch up and deep stalling – that characterised some other high performance aircraft of that period?

The first Avro 707, VX784, flew in September 1949 barely a year after the company received its order to build the Type 698 prototypes. Power was from a Rolls-Royce Derwent engine taken from a Meteor fighter, and wherever possible other parts were copied from existing aircraft. The air intake was unusual as it was a split dorsal intake in front of the fin.

BELOW VX790, the second of the flying scale models of the Avro 698 bomber, was invaluable in testing the low speed handling of the full-sized aircraft. *AHT*

Unfortunately the aircraft crashed a month later, killing its pilot. That was in the days before the installation of flight data recorders and the cause of the accident was never resolved conclusively.

The loss of the first Avro 707 imposed delays on the work on the second scale model, VX790, which began flying in August 1950. This aircraft, designated the Avro 707B, was designed to investigate the low speed handling characteristics of the delta wing. The nose was made longer and thinner than on the first 707, and the wing sweep angle was increased slightly. Also, the elevators and the air brakes were redesigned. However, like the first aircraft, the 707B had a dorsal air intake just in front of the fin. That intake position caused engine problems due to its location and its inability to cope with turbulent air streaming back from the cockpit canopy. Later the 707's air intake was repositioned but, even after this modification, it was never really satisfactory.

Roly Falk, a very experienced test pilot from the RAE, joined Avro at about this time. He flew the second Avro 707, and carried out the low speed handling trials which proved that the wing shape chosen for the Avro 698 was essentially satisfactory. One important contribution the Type 707 made to the Type 698 was that it showed the need for a longer nose undercarriage leg on the full-scale aircraft, to provide a greater wing incidence during the take-off run.

The first Avro 707 with representative air intakes, Avro 707A, WD280, flew in June 1951.

It was designed to fly at high sub-sonic speeds, and it pointed out the three main aerodynamic problems of the delta wing. Firstly, there was wing buffet and excessive drag at and above the cruising speed. Secondly, the aircraft was longitudinally unstable; as speed increased above the indicated cruising Mach number of Mach .85 the aircraft tried to dive. Above Mach .93 that dive became uncontrollable. Third and finally, the aircraft developed an uncontrollable short period pitching oscillation, when speed was increased above Mach .91. Avro solved the handling problems by using artificial stability aids. Today the use of such devices is routine, but at that time they were at the cutting edge of technology.

The buffeting and drag problems had to be solved aerodynamically, or the aircraft would not have met its performance specifications. It took much hard work, before a way was found to prevent the buffet and reduce the increase of drag. The solution was to fit a forward extension, outboard of the leading edge of the wing, with a pronounced droop. In addition, vortex generators were fitted to the top surface of the wing behind the modified leading edge, to delay separation of the boundary layer.

Two more Avro 707s were ordered in 1951, but in the event neither would be needed for the development of the Avro 698 and they were used in other programmes. Also during that year, prototypes of the two lowest risk heavy bomber types began test flying. The Vickers 660 made its maiden flight in May and the Short SA-4 followed in August.

ABOVE WD280, the third flying scale model to be built, had representative air intakes and was used to test handling at high speeds.

The prototype Vulcan pictured with its escort of four Avro 707s during 1953. *AHT*

Maiden flight

The prototype Avro 698, VX770, made its maiden flight on 30 August 1952 with Avro chief test pilot Roly Falk at the controls. The new Bristol BE 10 engine (later named the Olympus) was to have powered the aircraft, but it was still in the ground testing stage. Avro was determined to get its offering into the air before that of its Handley Page rival, so initially the Avro 698 was fitted with four 6,500lb thrust Rolls-Royce Avon engines. The only untoward incident during the maiden flight was that both undercarriage leg fairings broke away, and the aircraft flew without them in the days to follow.

The move stole the show and the big delta-winged bomber gained enormous welcome publicity. Meanwhile its Handley Page rival, still not ready for its maiden flight, languished on the ground at Boscombe Down.

Because of the reduced thrust of the Avon engines, the Avro 698 prototype was unable to reach the altitudes necessary to examine the aerodynamic problems encountered by the Avro 707A. However, there were several important new systems that could be tested lower down. These included the 112V direct current electrical system to power the flying controls, the fourteen tank fuel installation and the various hydraulic systems. The aircraft was also used to confirm the predicted benign low speed handling characteristics of the delta wing. Later the Avon engines were replaced by 7,500lb of thrust Armstrong Siddeley Sapphires, giving an extension of the bomber's performance envelope.

In October 1952 the Avro 698 was officially named the 'Vulcan', after the Roman god of fire and volcanic eruptions. The Vickers 660 had been christened the 'Valiant' a few months earlier. The Handley Page 80 first flew in December 1952 and it would be named the 'Victor'.

The second prototype Vulcan, VX777, made its first flight on 3 September 1953, fitted with the Bristol Olympus engines each developing 9,750lb of thrust. For a second year running the delta-winged bomber was the star of the Farnborough air show, when Avro put up an impressive formation with the two Vulcan prototypes flying in line astern, and a pair of Avro 707s on either flank.

During subsequent test flights, the second prototype was able to reach the representative operating altitudes necessary to examine the buffet boundaries and longitudinal instability of the aircraft. However, at this stage it had not yet been fitted with automatic stability aids.

The second prototype Vulcan nearly came to grief in July 1954, when its rudder jammed at full travel while in flight. Roly Falk made a skilful high speed landing at Farnborough in which the aircraft suffered serious damage. After some basic repairs, Falk flew the aircraft back to Woodford with the undercarriage down.

During 1955 Roly Falk took every opportunity to demonstrate the Vulcan's manoeuvrability before senior RAF officers, key politicians and the public. At the Farnborough air show that year he took the Prime Minister, Sir Anthony Eden, for a flight in the bomber. Also at that show he flew full barrel rolls in the aircraft, a move which attracted enormous publicity but also a firm rebuke to cease that practice.

Following repairs, the second prototype Vulcan next flew in October 1955 fitted with the modified drooped leading edge on the outer part of the wing. Tests confirmed that the modification improved the aircraft's handling at high sub-sonic

ABOVE AND LEFT These close-up air-to-air shots of the prototype Avro 698 show the advanced lines for its time of the new bomber. *AHT*

speeds, and it was satisfactory for incorporation in production aircraft. In addition the aircraft was fitted with a Mach trimmer and two pitch dampers, allowing tests to be carried out of handling at high Mach numbers.

BELOW The second prototype Avro 698, VX777, pictured in September 1953 at the Farnborough Air Show. *AHT*

Vulcan B1 – Leading Particulars

Crew:	5
Span:	99ft 0in
Length:	97ft 1in
Mainplane area:	3,554sq ft
Dihedral:	zero
Sweepback average:	45 degrees
Wing area:	3,554sq ft
Fin sweepback:	45 degrees
Height (top of fin):	26ft 6in
Track:	30ft
Engines:	4 x Bristol Olympus 101 turbojets of 11,000lb st; or Olympus 102 of 12,000lb st; or Olympus 104 of 13,000lb st
Normal maximum all-up weight:	167,000lb
Weight empty:	83,573lb
Maximum fuel, normal tankage:	9,250 imperial gallons, AVTUR 8lb per gallon, 73,760 lb
Performance:	maximum level speed Mach 0.95 (625mph) at 39,375ft; cruising speed Mach 0.92 (607mph) at 45,000ft; service ceiling 50,000ft; range 3,000 miles

Typical military loads
- 1 nuclear or thermonuclear bomb or
- up to twenty-one 1,000lb high explosive bombs

The B1 in production

The first production Vulcan, XA889, had flown in February 1955 powered by four Bristol Olympus engines each developing 11,000lb of thrust. Initially this aircraft was fitted with the original straight wings leading edge, but later it would be fitted with the production drooped leading edge. Tests confirmed that the revised wing shape, combined with the new auto stabilisers tested on the second prototype, were satisfactory. The aircraft was delivered to RAF Boscombe Down in March 1956 and received its certificate of airworthiness.

The first Vulcan delivered to the RAF was XA897, which arrived at Waddington in July 1956. This aircraft was destroyed in a tragic accident in the following October when it crashed at London Heathrow Airport in bad weather at the end of a round-the-world demonstration flight to Australia.

The first RAF unit to equip with 'The Flying Flatiron' was 83 Squadron based at Waddington, which started to receive aircraft of its own in July 1957. Altogether, forty-five Vulcan B1s were delivered between 1955 and 1959 and they formed the equipment of five front line units, 44, 50, 83, 101 and 617 Squadrons, and 230 Operational Conversion Unit (OCU). Like those in the rest of the V-Force, these aircraft were painted overall in brilliant anti-flash white, giving rise to the jibe that they belonged to 'the Detergent Force'.

During their time on Quick Reaction Alert (QRA) these aircraft were each loaded with a free-fall nuclear weapon, initially the British Blue Danube kiloton weapon, later replaced by the Violet Club, Yellow Sun megaton (British) weapons or the US Mk 5 weapon with a similar yield. In the late 1960s the WE177B free-fall thermonuclear bomb replaced all other weapons of this type. Even now, fifty years later, it is difficult to obtain reliable and detailed information on these weapons. A Yellow Sun shape is exhibited at the RAF Museum, Cosford.

The aircraft were also fitted with in-flight refuelling capability to extend their global reach. To demonstrate the effectiveness of that capability a Vulcan of 617 Squadron flew non-stop from RAF Scampton to Sydney, Australia, on June 20/21 June 1961.

It covered the distance in 20 hours and 5 minutes, having taken fuel from nine Valiant tankers along the route.

Enter the B2

Meanwhile, Rolls-Royce had taken over Bristol Siddeley engines, and development of the Olympus engine continued. The Olympus 104 produced a maximum of 13,000lb of thrust, while the redesigned Olympus 200 Series engine developed 17,000lb of thrust. The Vulcan B1 wing was unable to exploit the increased power developed by the new engine at high altitude, however, due to the excessive drag and buffeting encountered at the higher wing angles of attack. To get the full benefit from the higher engine thrust levels now available, in 1954 Avro was contracted to produce an improved B2 version. This would have a redesigned wing of greater area, as well as several other new features.

ABOVE The mighty Yellow Sun megaton thermonuclear weapon equipped several Vulcan B2 free-fall squadrons. The weapon took up almost the whole of the Vulcan's bomb bay (the standard lorry-type wheels give an indication of scale).

BELOW To demonstrate the effectiveness of the Vulcan's in-flight refuelling capability, on 20–21 June 1961 an aircraft of No 617 Squadron flew non-stop from RAF Scampton to Sydney, Australia. It covered the distance in just over 20 hours, having taken fuel from nine Valiant tankers along the route.

ABOVE Co-author
Tony Blackman
demonstrates XA891,
the first production
Vulcan B1, at the 1958
Farnborough Air Show.

The second prototype Vulcan served as a development aircraft to test new features to be incorporated in the B2, and the much-modified aircraft resumed flying in August 1957. It had a larger wing, the span increased by 12ft and the wing area increased by 410sq ft. In place of the four ailerons and four elevators operating separately, as on the B1, there were now eight control surfaces – elevons – which operated in both the aileron and the elevator senses

as required. Also, to feed the more powerful engines, the aircraft had its air intakes enlarged.

To enhance the Vulcan B2's ability to penetrate the enemy defences and reach its war targets, the aircraft was to be fitted with an electronic countermeasures (ECM) suite which included a battery of high powered noise jammers (these systems are described in Chapter 6). To provide the very large amounts of electrical power required to run these systems, the aircraft's electrical generation system was changed from 112 volt direct current system of the B1, to a state-of-the-art 200 volt 400 cycles alternating current system on the B2. The system employed four large engine-driven alternators, with a Ram Air Turbine (RAT) and an Auxiliary Airborne Power Plant (AAPP) as back-ups. These systems are described in greater detail in Chapter 3. The development work for the new electrical system was carried out on a Vulcan B1, XA893. To dissipate the large amount of heat thus generated, the aircraft carried an electrical load mat in the bomb bay nicknamed 'The toast rack'.

To ensure surge-free engine handling at high altitudes, the new Olympus 200 series engines for the B2 required several modifications. This work was carried out using Vulcan B1, XA891. It proved to be a lengthy process since the engine controls at that time were analogue systems, very large and cumbersome. Moreover, the mechanical modules which sensed pressures and controlled fuel flows were awkward to adjust.

Another problem was that with the common air intake for both engines on each side, if one engine surged and flamed out at high altitude, the adjacent engine invariably failed as well. To relight these engines above 35,000ft a 'hot relight' was required; it was necessary to press the engine relight buttons *immediately* and slowly close the throttles. If a relight on an engine was going to be successful the jet pipe temperature would start to rise and the RPM would stop falling and then begin to increase. If no satisfactory relight occurred then the HP cock would need to be closed and the altitude

LEFT Vulcan XH533, the first Vulcan B2, is demonstrated at the Farnborough Air Show in September 1958.

would have to be reduced to below 35,000ft. After a pause to allow the engine to drain, the HP cock would be re-opened, the relight button pressed and the throttle slowly opened until the JPT and RPM started to rise.

The first production Vulcan B2 flew on 19 August 1958. Deliveries to the RAF commenced on 1 July 1960 when co-author Tony Blackman flew Vulcan XH558 – of which more later – to 230 OCU at Waddington.

Meanwhile the Vulcan B1s in service also underwent several upgrades. They were fitted with the more powerful Olympus Mk 104 engine developing 13,000lb of thrust. To enhance the Vulcan B1's ability to reach its targets, these aircraft were later fitted with the same electronic countermeasures suite as the B2, with the same bulged tail fairing to accommodate them (see Chapter 6). Vulcan B1s so modified were re-designated as Vulcan B1As.

ABOVE The Vulcan B1A was a Mk 1 modified to carry the full suite of ECM equipment, and fitted with a bleed-air turbine to generate the necessary electrical power to drive these systems. This particular aircraft, XA907, served for some time with the Bomber Command Development Unit at RAF Finningley, where it was used to test the ECM and other systems due to be fitted to the B2.

LEFT A staged RAF publicity photograph of a Vulcan B1A at RAF Waddington, taken at night to show that getting a Vulcan into the air was a team effort.

RIGHT XA903, a Vulcan B1, was used during the initial carrying and release trials of the Blue Steel missile over the Aberporth range in west Wales.

Blue Steel

In parallel with the Mk 2 V-bomber programme, the RAF had placed an order with Avro to design and build an air-to-surface missile to provide a stand-off attack capability for Mk 2 V-bombers. Designated Blue Steel, the weapon was 35ft long, it had a stub wing with a span of 13ft and at launch it weighed 17,000lb. The missile had a maximum effective range of about 100 nautical miles if launched at altitudes around 48,000ft, or about half that distance if it was launched at low altitude. The missile carried a Violet Club megaton range thermonuclear warhead, and it navigated itself to its target using a built-in inertial guidance system.

Blue Steel was powered by a de Havilland (later Bristol Siddeley) Stentor liquid fuelled rocket motor fitted with two combustion chambers. During the initial part of its flight, running on its main combustion chamber, the Stentor developed 16,000lb of thrust. This carried the weapon to 70,000ft and accelerated it to around Mach 2.5. Then the main combustion chamber cut out and the secondary chamber cut in, producing 4,000lb of thrust to sustain the weapon at that altitude and speed. Near the end of its four-minute flight-time the missile bunted into its terminal dive to penetrate the target's defences at a speed of around Mach 1.8.

RIGHT Preparing Blue Steel at RAF Scampton in 1964. The service personnel fuelling the weapon wear flame-retardant clothing to protect them from the highly corrosive nature of HTP (High Test Peroxide).
IWM RAFT3595

RIGHT A view of the underside of a Vulcan B2 of the Scampton Wing showing the fitted Blue Steel weapon. The Scampton Wing consisted of Nos 27, 83 and 617 Squadrons. A safety suited technician fuels the Blue Steel. In the background XM571 can be seen undergoing pre-flight preparations. *IWM RAFT4841*

In service, the Blue Steel required very careful handling. The Stentor ran on kerosene (80 gallons) and High Test Peroxide (HTP, 400 gallons). When these two fuels came together the HTP decomposed with great violence to produce thrust. The trouble was, the HTP was highly likely to decompose in that way if it came into contact with almost any form of impurity. Near-surgical standards of cleanliness were therefore required when the HTP was transported, and the liquid had to be kept in airtight containers at all times. Any accident that brought together the nuclear material in the warhead with the HTP could produce a powerful chemical explosion. And while such an explosion would not assume nuclear proportions, it was likely to spread radioactive contamination over a large area.

To reduce the chances of that to a minimum, peacetime safety considerations precluded the routine loading of aircraft with ready-to-launch Blue Steel missiles. When a Blue Steel aircraft went on QRA (on the ground) it had the missile fitted in its bomb bay, but the weapon was without its load of HTP. From the order to take off, it would take more than half an hour to fuel the missile and complete the other necessary preparations. Only in the event of national emergency could these precautions be lifted.

ABOVE Blue Steel is loaded onto Vulcan B2, XM571, at RAF Scampton in 1964. *IWM RAFT4855*

BELOW Vulcan B2, XL384, of the Scampton Wing, carrying a Blue Steel practice round over Niagara Falls in North America during a Blue Steel training mission in about 1970. *IWM RAFT5887*

OPPOSITE Alone and at high altitude – a Vulcan in its element. This example is a B2A of No 27 Squadron, carrying a Blue Steel training round beneath the fuselage. *AHT*

The first operational unit to receive the Vulcan B2 was 83 Squadron based at Scampton, soon followed by 27 and 617 Squadrons. Initially these units carried the British Yellow Sun Mk 2 free-fall thermonuclear weapon, but in the autumn of 1962 they began to re-equip with the Vulcan B2A modified to carry Blue Steel.

The planned replacement for Blue Steel was the US-manufactured Douglas Skybolt air-launched ballistic missile (see Skybolt text box). This weapon performed badly in tests, however, and the US government cancelled its further development. In its place the British government accepted a US offer to sell it the Polaris submarine-launched ballistic missile, to be carried by Royal Navy submarines. From then on, the days of the RAF's tenure of the nation's nuclear deterrent were numbered.

RIGHT AND BELOW What might have been: B2, XH537, fitted with a pair of dummy Douglas Skybolt air-launched ballistic missiles mounted under the wings. The RAF planned to order the weapon from the US as a replacement for the Blue Steel missile, but the Skybolt had a troubled development phase. Eventually the US government decided to cancel the programme. *PRM Aviation*

Skybolt

The Douglas Skybolt was an air-launched ballistic missile designed in the late 1950s for carriage by manned aircraft. The weapon weighed about 11,000lb, measured 38ft 6in long and had a diameter of 35in. The US Air Force's Boeing B-52 strategic bomber was to carry four of these missiles on under-wing launchers.

Skybolt was powered by an Aerojet two-stage solid fuelled rocket, and was to carry a W59 thermonuclear warhead. Navigation was by means of inertial platform. After launch the rocket lifted the missile to an altitude of about 300 nautical miles, then it followed a ballistic trajectory to its target. The weapon was designed to have maximum range of about 1,000 nautical miles.

The RAF joined the Skybolt programme in 1960, with the intention of fitting two of these weapons under the wings of modified Vulcan B2s. In tests the missile performed badly, however, and its first five launches were all considered to be failures. The programme was cancelled in 1963.

A Skybolt missile shape is on exhibition at the RAF Museum at Cosford

The crew of a Vulcan B2 of No 27 Squadron at RAF Scampton leave their aircraft after a high altitude training sortie. Each man wears a partial pressure jerkin, with a built-in yellow life jacket. The modified anti-G suit trousers are worn inside the flying overalls and cannot be seen.

Escape and survival at extreme altitude

The Vulcan B2 was designed to fly strike missions at altitudes of 56,000ft and above. If at that altitude the pressurisation failed or the cabin was pierced, for example by fragments from a missile detonating nearby, a man lacking suitable protection would face death from three separate causes, all working against him simultaneously. He would die from lack of oxygen (even breathing 100 per cent oxygen via a normal mask would not save him), from the intense cold (minus 56 degrees C) and from the multiple and uniformly unpleasant effects of decompression sickness. These were the bends – pains arising from joints in the limbs which progressed into more severe pains spreading up and down the affected limbs; the creeps – a tingling feeling usually in the thighs and trunk; and the chokes, characterised by a burning feeling in the chest with pain on breathing in, often accompanied by a severe bouts of dry coughing.

The crew required special clothing to survive such an emergency. Each man wore a special tight-fitting pressure breathing oxygen mask, a partial pressure jerkin and a tight fitting anti-G suit. The purpose of the anti-G suit covering the legs was not to increase the wearer's tolerance to the effects of 'G'. In this case the garment had been modified to prevent blood being forced from the wearer's trunk into his legs when the jerkin inflated, thereby negating the pressure breathing process.

With all that extra clothing there was a risk that the wearer would suffer heat stress, especially if the aircraft was held on the ground at stand-by for long periods on a hot day. To overcome that potential problem each crewman wore a nylon air ventilated suit as an undergarment. This garment covered the wearer's arms, legs and trunk and had stitched into it more than thirty small-bore pipes to convey cool air to the various parts of the body.

In the event of a blow out at high altitude,

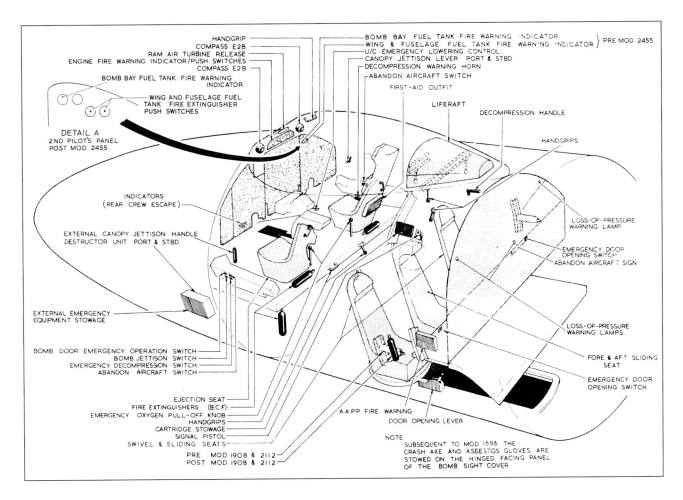

DETAIL A
2ND PILOT'S PANEL
POST MOD. 2455

HANDGRIP
COMPASS E2B
RAM AIR TURBINE RELEASE
ENGINE FIRE WARNING INDICATOR/PUSH SWITCHES
COMPASS E2B
BOMB BAY FUEL TANK FIRE WARNING
INDICATOR
WING AND FUSELAGE FUEL
TANK FIRE EXTINGUISHER
PUSH SWITCHES

BOMB BAY FUEL TANK FIRE WARNING INDICATOR
WING & FUSELAGE FUEL TANK FIRE WARNING INDICATOR } PRE MOD. 2455
U/C EMERGENCY LOWERING CONTROL
CANOPY JETTISON LEVER PORT & STBD
DECOMPRESSION WARNING HORN
ABANDON AIRCRAFT SWITCH
FIRST-AID OUTFIT
LIFERAFT
DECOMPRESSION HANDLE
HANDGRIPS

INDICATORS
(REAR CREW ESCAPE)

EXTERNAL CANOPY JETTISON HANDLE
DESTRUCTOR UNIT PORT & STBD.

EXTERNAL EMERGENCY
EQUIPMENT STOWAGE

BOMB DOOR EMERGENCY OPERATION SWITCH
BOMB JETTISON SWITCH
EMERGENCY DECOMPRESSION SWITCH
ABANDON AIRCRAFT SWITCH

EJECTION SEAT
FIRE EXTINGUISHERS (B.C.F)
EMERGENCY OXYGEN PULL-OFF KNOB
HANDGRIPS
CARTRIDGE STOWAGE
SIGNAL PISTOL
SWIVEL & SLIDING SEATS
PRE MOD. 1908 & 2112
POST MOD. 1908 & 2112

LOSS-OF-PRESSURE
WARNING LAMP
EMERGENCY DOOR
OPENING SWITCH
ABANDON AIRCRAFT SIGN

LOSS-OF-PRESSURE
WARNING LAMPS
FORE & AFT SLIDING
SEAT
EMERGENCY DOOR
OPENING SWITCH

A.A.P.P. FIRE WARNING
DOOR OPENING LEVER

NOTE
SUBSEQUENT TO MOD. 1696 THE
CRASH AXE AND ASBESTOS GLOVES ARE
STOWED ON THE HINGED FACING PANEL
OF THE BOMB SIGHT COVER

each man's oxygen mask, jerkin and anti-G suit inflated with oxygen under pressure. That process, practised on the ground from time to time in a decompression chamber, was an uncomfortable experience. When the pressure was released with a loud bang, the occupants were at a notional altitude of 56,000ft. The sudden misting up of the chamber was disconcerting, though that soon cleared. Then each man's lungs filled with oxygen under pressure, which made breathing out hard work. On the intercom, the sounds of loud heavy breathing gave the impression that the crew was having a far more enjoyable time than was in fact the case!

The aim was to maintain consciousness for long enough to bring the aircraft down to 25,000ft or below, where the outside air environment was a good deal less hostile. Then the crew could abandon the aircraft if necessary, or continue with the mission if possible.

In the event, none of this ever happened.

Nobody ever needed to abandon a Vulcan at very high altitude, so the escape system was never put to the test.

The switch to low altitude

Meanwhile, Britain's V-Force had come under other pressures. In May 1960 a Lockheed U-2 high altitude reconnaissance plane, flown by CIA pilot Gary Powers, was shot down near Sverdlovsk deep inside the Soviet Union. Reportedly the aircraft was flying at an altitude of around 67,000ft when it was hit. The aircraft had been engaged by an S-75 (NATO code name SA-2) surface-to-air missile battery. It had been hoped that the V-bombers' high altitude attack capability, coupled with the use of ECM protection, would preserve their deterrent effect at least into the mid-1960s. However, the U-2 shoot-down demonstrated that Soviet anti-aircraft missile technology had advanced rather more rapidly than expected. At the same

ABOVE High altitude escape – emergency controls and equipment.

BELOW The occasion for this three-aircraft Vulcan formation was the granting of the Freedom of Boston, Lincolnshire, to RAF Coningsby in June 1963. The aircraft came from each of the station's three resident units, Nos 9, 12, and 35 Squadrons. After the fly past over Boston, the leading Vulcan set course westward to convey a letter of greetings from the mayor of the British town to his counterpart in Boston, Massachusetts, USA. *Alfred Price collection*

time, the number of S-75 batteries deployed around potential targets in the Soviet Union increased with each month that passed, giving the bombers progressively less opportunity to employ evasive routeing to avoid the defences.

The answer was to switch the V-Force from a high altitude to a low altitude penetration of enemy territory to its targets. The Valiant force was the first part to abandon the high level penetration tactic, when they moved to a 'hi-lo-hi' attack mode in 1961. Next to make the transition was the B1 and B1A Vulcans and Victors, which began training in the new tactics in March 1963. Finally the Vulcan B2s and the Victors made the changeover in the spring of 1964.

Before the change to the low level mode of penetration, V-Force aircraft were still painted in white gloss overall. With the transition to low altitude operations these aircraft became highly visible when observed from above. The RAF ran a crash programme to repaint the upper surfaces

of these aircraft in a disruptive grey/green camouflage pattern, although initially they retained their anti-flash white on the lower surfaces.

As mentioned earlier, from early in 1962 the Vulcan B2s delivered to the RAF had their wings strengthened and modified, to enable them to carry a couple of Skybolt air-launched ballistic missiles. When this weapon was cancelled the RAF told Avro to continue to embody these modifications. Those strengthened wings would now serve a quite different purpose, giving a useful increase in the aircraft's fatigue life when they were committed to flying in the turbulent air at low altitude.

No such modification would be applied to the Victor or the Valiant, however. In August 1964 one of the latter suffered a mid-air failure of the wing rear spar, and the crew was indeed fortunate to get it back on the ground without further damage to the aircraft or to themselves. Examination of the spar revealed a major metal

fatigue failure, which several other Valiants were close to replicating. The entire fleet had to be grounded and these aircraft never flew again.

The active life of the Valiant had been barely twelve years. The aircraft had originally been ordered as the least risky 'backstop' design of the three V bomber types that entered service. Yet, remarkably, it proved to have the shortest fatigue life of them all.

Escape from the Vulcan at medium and low altitudes

Each of the three V-bomber types carried a crew of five, of which only the two pilots had ejection seats. The procedure for abandoning a V-bomber in an emergency at low or medium altitude (up to 40,000ft) was therefore for the pilots to keep the aircraft in the air for long enough for the three rear crew members to escape. Then the pilots would eject.

In the case of the Vulcan, the entrance door also served as the emergency escape chute for the rear crew members. That escape chute was positioned in front of the nose undercarriage leg, it was important that the undercarriage be retracted before the rear crew members attempted to escape. In case this was not possible, the rear crew members regularly practised a procedure for use in this eventuality. As the escapee slid down the chute, he grabbed one of the chute door jacks. That would shift his body sufficiently far to that side to carry him clear of the nose wheel leg. Fortunately that procedure never had to be tested in a real emergency.

How well did the Vulcan's escape systems work in practice? In all, fifteen Vulcans were lost in crashes. These were spread over 31½ years, from the first flight of the prototype to the Vulcan's withdrawal from front line service. In five cases all the crew members bailed out successfully, so the lack of ejection seats for the rear crew made no difference to their survival chances. In a further six cases none of the crew survived so, again, the lack of ejection seats for the rear crew probably made no difference to their survival chances. In the remaining four cases, the pilots ejected but the rear crew members were unable to escape from the aircraft and all were killed. So, arguably, had those rear crew members had ejection seats some or all of them might have survived (source: Tony Blackman, *Vulcan Test Pilot*).

In summary, although the escape provisions in the Vulcan were not ideal, considering that its in-service period covered most of the Cold War, the risks could be considered acceptable for a front line military aircraft.

ABOVE Bad day at RAF Finningley, 18 April 1966. The crew had boarded XH556 and begun the pre-engine start checks, when a freak electrical fault initiated the undercarriage retraction sequence. The main wheels started to fold and for a brief time the nose wheel leg bore much of the weight of the Vulcan, before the structure collapsed and broke the back of the aircraft. One of the pilots jettisoned the cockpit canopy and the crew made hasty if undignified exits by sliding down the nose. Fortunately nobody was hurt, but the aircraft never flew again.

Improved capability

In all, 89 Vulcan B2s were built and they formed the equipment of eight frontline units: 9, 12, 27, 35, 44, 50, 101 and 617 Squadrons and 230 OCU. The last of these aircraft, XM657, was delivered to the RAF in January 1965.

Throughout its service career the Vulcan B2 underwent numerous incremental improvements. One such was the installation of 21,000lb of thrust Olympus 301 engines fitted with the rapid start capability. Initially the Vulcan B2 started its engines one at a time. The rapid start capability (described in detail in Chapter 3) employed very high pressure air to start all four engines simultaneously, thereby shaving more than a minute off the time needed to get a four-aircraft flight of bombers airborne on a scramble take-off.

Another important addition was the fitting of the terrain following radar (TFR) in the extreme nose of the aircraft, to enable it to fly safely at lower altitudes than previously. Then there were the improvements to the ECM suite. There was a new and more capable radar warning receiver to replace Blue Saga, an I-Band jamming system to counter fighter airborne interception (AI) and missile guidance radars, and an infra red (IR) decoy dispenser fitted in place of one of the chaff containers. There was also the Red Steer Mk 2 tail warning radar, which was sensitive enough to detect a missile approaching in the bomber's rear quarter in time to dispense IR decoys or chaff (see Chapter 6 for more details).

The Vulcan continued to operate in the nuclear deterrent role until 30 June 1969, when the Royal Navy's new Polaris ballistic missile submarines took over that task. With that move

OPPOSITE The Battle of Britain Memorial Flight Avro Lancaster passes over four Avro Vulcan B2s of 230 OCU on the ORP (Operational Readiness Platform) at RAF Waddington in March 1968. The Vulcan B2s are (front to rear) XH561, XJ782, XM656 and XJ824. The fly past marked the amalgamation of Bomber and Fighter Commands and the creation of Strike Command.
IWM RAFT8296

LEFT Emitting a dense cloud of black smoke and an ear-splitting roar from the four Olympus engines running at full power, a Vulcan B2 gets airborne.

ABOVE With air
brakes in the high
drag position, a Vulcan
B2 is seen on finals
to touchdown at
RAF Waddington in
November 1982.
Ian Black

RIGHT With a screech
of tortured rubber
and a puff of smoke,
a Vulcan from 230
OCU announces its
touchdown.

The Chinese connection

An unusual role assigned to 27 Squadron in March 1975 was that of monitoring Chinese nuclear tests – Operation 'Aroma'. The AEO leader on the unit, Squadron Leader Peter West, recalled:

'The intelligence guys would be watching for signs that the Chinese were about to run another test. When a test seemed imminent three Vulcan crews, two Vulcans and a supporting VC10 would hot-foot it out to Midway Island in the Pacific, something like 11,000 miles from Scampton. It would take us four days to get there, staging through Goose Bay in Canada, Offutt in Nebraska, McLelland in California then out to Midway. Each detachment took with it a boffin from the Atomic Energy Research Establishment at Aldermaston, who assessed our findings.

'There was also a meteorological expert from Bracknell, to observe the wind patterns and ascertain the best area in which to search for nuclear dust in the upper atmosphere. After taking off from Midway we would head north-north-west to search for the nuclear debris. We had a fair success rate, but given the huge area of the Pacific we had to search, I think it was remarkable that we had any success at all.

'The under wing air sampling pods were conventional streamlined pods, modified Sea Vixen drop tanks. Inside each there was a Geiger counter, operated by the AEO. When the Geiger counter detected radioactive fallout, the AEO operated a switch to open the front of the pod to expose a filter paper resembling a piece of blotting paper about the size of a saucer. That picked up whatever we found, it was very simple and straightforward.

'When we landed we all had to be checked over with a Geiger counter. To the best of my knowledge no one was ever contaminated. It seems the radioactivity was attenuated considerably by the time we found it. When we returned to the UK we were debriefed, and we were told whether we had brought back anything useful. The extraordinary thing was that from that little piece of paper, the boffins could tell the materials used in the bomb and its yield. All told I flew on three "Aroma" detachments, 12 to 25 March 1975, 9 August to 16 September 1975 and 24 January to 2 February 1976.'

LEFT Offutt Air Force Base, Nebraska, USA, 19 May 1968. Co-author Alfred Price was the AEO onboard XH559 when it flew its display before an appreciative American audience.

ABOVE XM647 served with the RAF Near East Bomber Wing based at Akrotiri, Cyprus, from January 1969 to January 1975. The small radome in the extreme nose, just beneath the refuelling probe, belongs to the terrain following radar.

RIGHT XM647 pictured on her landing approach. Note the additional fuel tank in the forward end of the bomb bay.

the three Vulcan Blue Steel units, 27, 83 and 617 Squadrons, ceased standing on QRA. In the following year these units gave up their Blue Steel modified aircraft, which were returned to the free-fall bombing role.

With the removal of the Vulcan's nuclear deterrent task, some of these aircraft could be redeployed. In January 1969 two units, 9 and 35 Squadrons, moved to Akrotiri in Cyprus where they replaced the Canberras in the Near East Air Force Bomber Wing. The deployment lasted until January 1975, when both units returned to England. No 9 Squadron moved to Waddington where it remained until it was disbanded in April 1982, while 35 Squadron went to Scampton until it, too, was disbanded in the same month.

Reconnaissance role

With the reduction in the Vulcan's nuclear role, 27 Squadron was disbanded in March 1972. Just over a year later, in November 1973, the unit reformed in the maritime reconnaissance role with four Vulcan B2s, later increased to eight. Squadron Leader Peter West, Air Electronics Operator (AEO) leader on the unit, recalled:

'The Maritime Radar Reconnaissance made a pleasant change from the usual Vulcan thing, of flying over the UK and dropping imaginary bombs on imaginary targets. Our role was to relieve the Nimrods from carrying out a surface search, thus allowing them to concentrate on their anti-submarine role. We had very good radar, we would get up to our normal Vulcan altitudes, around 40,000ft, and in a couple of sorties we could cover the entire North Atlantic. We would signal to the maritime headquarters all the surface contacts we picked up. If we found a few ships operating close together, and they were not NATO vessels, the chances were they were Soviet ships. In time of war, we might have homed in a Buccaneer striking force to attack them.'

BELOW XM645 is seen here making a high-speed run at low altitude.

By the summer of 1981 the Vulcan was nearing the end of its service life. Its planned replacement, the Panavia Tornado, was starting to come off the production lines in useful numbers. The phased rundown of the Vulcan force commenced that August and the first unit to go was 230 OCU. By the following April 9, 27, 35 and 617 Squadrons had joined it. Then the process came to a precipitate halt, following the Argentine invasion of the Falkland Islands in April 1982. The Vulcan operations during that conflict are described in detail in the next chapter.

Tanker Vulcans

The ultra-long range operations flown during the Falklands conflict placed a huge load on the Victor tanker force, and the RAF cast around for a way to get 'more hoses in the sky'. The only large aircraft type that was readily available was the Vulcan, and six of these aircraft were selected for modification to the tanker role. This conversion involved removing the ECM blister and equipments in the tail, and replacing them with a Flight Refuelling Mk 17B hose drum unit. To increase the aircraft's fuel carrying ability, three 1,000-gallon auxiliary fuel tanks were installed in the bomb bay.

XH561, the first Vulcan K2, arrived at the Woodford works on 4 May 1982 and resumed flying on completion of the modifications on 18 June – four days after the Argentine troops on the Falklands surrendered. With the end of the Falklands conflict, the phased rundown of the Vulcan force resumed. No 101 Squadron disbanded in August 1982. That left 44 Squadron the last remaining Vulcan bomber unit, and it went in December. In the airborne tanking role 50 Squadron soldiered on until March 1984, when it went the way of all the others.

ABOVE XH558 pictured after her modification for the tanker role.

I thought: 'That's clever, how did they do that?' – Squadron Leader Peter West

In the RAF, operational crews are required to undergo periodic tests of proficiency in the air, from a team of experts in the operation of their particular aircraft. Throughout the RAF these teams are known, with a mixture of respect and trepidation, as 'Trappers'. Squadron Leader Peter West of 27 Squadron recalled a memorable Trappers' sortie, in XH558 of all aircraft, on 6 November 1975:

'I was flying with my crew, captain Squadron Leader John Porter, on a Trapper ride. With that type of sortie there was often a simulated double-engine failure on take-off. That was to be expected. We went rolling down the runway and lifted off, then suddenly there was a loud bang. I thought "That's clever, how did they do that?" They didn't. It turned out a large bird had gone down the starboard inner air intake. The engine blew up causing debris to enter the starboard outer engine intake, which blew up also. We had quite a serious fire and we began preparations to jump out. For the only time in my 35-year flying career, I made an emergency call prefixed by "Mayday, Mayday, Mayday". But then the pilots did a marvellous job and got us back on the ground safely. Poor old 558 was in the "hospital" for several months for repairs. Which is probably why she had a lot more flying time left on her than any of the other Vulcans when the squadrons disbanded.'

THIS PAGE A pair of Phantoms from No 19 Squadron, RAF Germany, take on fuel from Vulcan B (K) 2, XL445, in September 1982. *Ian Black*

ABOVE The final role for the Vulcan was as a tanker. Vulcan B (K) 2, XH560, on the right, is fitted with a hose drum unit in place of the ECM blister.

LEFT The RAF took delivery of its first Vulcan B1 the month after the last RAF Spitfire unit (the Meteorological Flight at Woodvale, flying the PR19) disbanded in June 1957. This is the Battle of Britain Flight's Spitfire PR19, PS853, alongside Vulcan B2, XH558.
Vulcan to the Sky Trust

'Air power is a thunderbolt
launched from an egg-shell invisibly
tethered to a base.'
Hoffman Nickerson

Chapter 2

When the Vulcan Went to War

The Vulcan served in the RAF for more than a quarter of a century, yet it was only in the twilight of its service career that it finally went into action. At the beginning of April 1982, Argentine military forces invaded the Falkland Islands and South Georgia in the South Atlantic, and quickly seized both territories. As the British government explored the diplomatic options for recovering the islands, selected Army, Navy and RAF units received orders to begin preparations to retrieve the islands by force, should this prove necessary. The ensuing military operation was called Operation 'Corporate'.

OPPOSITE On gilded wings: Vulcan B2, XH558. *Damien Burke*

At RAF Waddington, the last remaining operational Vulcan base, 44, 50 and 101 Squadrons were well advanced in their preparations to disband during the first few weeks of April 1982. Now these arrangements suddenly gave way to a more serious task. Wing Commander Simon Baldwin, commanding officer of 44 Squadron, was ordered to open a planning cell in the station's operations centre, to explore the possibility of using the Vulcan to fly operations over the South Atlantic. The planned series of operations received the codename 'Black Buck'.

Such an enterprise would face huge difficulties. The nearest air base to the Falklands, that was available to the British forces, was Wideawake airfield on Ascension Island. But to attack targets in the Falklands from there would involve a round trip of 7,700 miles, or about as far as from London to Karachi and back. If it took place, it would be the longest range bombing attack in the history of aerial warfare.

BELOW Vulcan XM607 on the ground at Wideawake airfield.

As a preliminary step, Baldwin ordered the refurbishment of the in-flight refuelling systems of six Vulcans, after more than a decade of disuse. Then the selected Vulcan crews began to practise taking fuel from Victor tankers, something which most of them had never attempted before.

When diplomacy failed

As April 1982 drew to a close, it was clear that diplomacy alone would not resolve the Falklands crisis. Two specially prepared Vulcans arrived at Wideawake, each loaded with twenty-one 1,000lb bombs. Their crews had been briefed to bomb Port Stanley airfield during the small hours of 1 May. One Vulcan was to fly the mission; the other would serve as an airborne reserve in case the primary aircraft went unserviceable. To support the attack there would be no fewer than eleven Victor tankers, including two airborne reserves.

With such an important and complex

military operation, there is often a dress rehearsal beforehand in an area remote from the conflict, to iron out as many of the problems as possible. In the case of the 'Black Buck' operation, however, there was no such rehearsal. Squadron Leader Bob Tuxford, one of the Victor tanker captains, explained: 'It would have been as much trouble to run a rehearsal as to fly the mission, so it was decided to fly the mission. If the problems had become too great, we would have broken off the mission and called it the rehearsal.'

The raiders and their supporting tankers began taking off from Wideawake at 22.50hrs Ascension Time (19.50hrs Port Stanley Time) on 30 April. At one-minute intervals the heavily laden aircraft thundered down the runway and disappeared into the night sky. Events soon confirmed the wisdom of sending the airborne reserves. During the climb-out, the cabin of the primary bombing Vulcan failed to pressurise, and one Victor tanker was unable to reel out its refuelling hose. Both aircraft had to abandon the mission.

'Looks like we've got a job of work, fellers ...'

Flight Lieutenant Martin Withers was captain of the reserve Vulcan. When he heard that the primary bomber was forced to abort the mission, there was a pregnant silence on the intercom. Then Withers piped up: 'Looks like we've got a job of work, fellers ...' No further discussion was necessary, for the reserve crew had briefed for the mission as assiduously as those now forced to abandon it.

About 840 miles south of Ascension, the first part of the complex fuel transfer began. The operation could be likened to a huge relay race, but instead of batons the aircraft passed thousands of gallons of aviation kerosene between each other. Four Victors passed all their spare fuel to four others, then turned back for Ascension. Another Victor then topped up the Vulcan's tanks.

The Vulcan and the Victors flew in loose formation at 30,000ft, the optimum cruising

BELOW Vulcan and Victor crews listen intently during a briefing at Wideawake airfield, Ascension Island, before a 'Black Buck' mission.

altitude for the tankers. That was 10,000ft lower than the optimum altitude of the Vulcan, which meant the latter consumed fuel at a slightly higher rate than planned. The resultant shortfall could come only from the reserves carried by the individual Victor tankers.

Two and a half hours after take-off, about 1,150 miles from Ascension, the second fuel transfer took place. Three Victors topped up the fuel tanks of three others and the Vulcan, and then turned back. One and a half hours after that, about 1,900 miles south of Ascension, came the third fuel transfer.

Meanwhile, at Wideawake airfield, there were tense scenes as the four Victors returned from the first refuelling transfer. The tankers arrived simultaneously, all of them low on fuel. The airfield's single east-west runway could be entered or left only at its western end. And, as luck would have it, the wind was blowing from the east. That meant the Victors would finish their landing runs at the end furthest from the exit. The normal procedure then would have been for each aircraft to land, turn around, back

ABOVE The crew of XM607 during the first 'Black Buck' operation photographed beside their aircraft. From left to right: Flt Lt Martin Withers (captain); Flt Lt Bob Wright (radar navigator); Flg Off Peter Taylor (co-pilot); Flt Lt Gordon Graham (navigator plotter); and Flt Lt Hugh Prior (AEO). *Martin Withers*

BELOW A Victor tanker lands at Wideawake, streaming its braking parachute. Eleven of these aircraft supported the first 'Black Buck' mission.

track the runway and get clear before the next aircraft touched down. But if the Victors did that, there was a risk that one of them might run out of fuel before it could land.

Given that certainty, the tanker crews took the least-bad alternative. The first Victor touched down, ran to the end of the runway and stopped. The second aircraft landed and pulled up behind the first. The third tanker landed and pulled up behind the second. When Squadron Leader Martin Todd touched down in the fourth Victor, the stage was set for the aeronautical equivalent of a motorway pile-up. Any misjudgment by the pilot, or a relatively minor technical malfunction in the aircraft, might result in the loss of four irreplaceable Victor tankers and their crews. As Todd touched down he could see the other three tankers sitting on the runway in front of him, anti-collision lights blinking in the darkness. He streamed his braking parachute and felt a reassuring tug on his straps as the Victor slowed rapidly. Later Todd commented: 'There were the other three at the end of the runway, waiting for us to stop. If our brakes had failed or anything, Christ, I hate to think of it ...'

But there was no failure. Todd halted short of the other aircraft, turned through a semi-circle and taxied towards the runway exit. In relieved procession, the other three tankers followed.

'It was dreadfully turbulent...'

By now the force heading south comprised just two Victors and the single attack Vulcan. Five and a half hours and some 2,700 miles after take-off, there was a further transfer of fuel. And now a new problem arose. Squadron Leader Bob Tuxford, captain of one of the Victors, explained: 'There is an unwritten rule in air-to-air refuelling, a variation of Sod's law, which says if you're going to find any really bumpy weather, it will be right at the point where you have to do your tanking. That proved to be the case and the "really bumpy weather" duly appeared as a violent tropical storm at exactly the point where the final transfer of fuel between the Victors was planned to take place.'

From his Vulcan, Martin Withers watched Flight Lieutenant Steve Biglands close in on Tuxford's aircraft and try to receive fuel. 'It was dreadfully

ABOVE A Victor tanker streams its three refuelling hoses. When refuelling a large aircraft like a Vulcan, only the centre-line hose was used.
Alfred Price collection

turbulent, we were in and out of the cloud tops. There was a lot of electrical activity, with St Elmo's fire dancing around the cockpit. The Victor was trying to refuel in that, he was having enormous problems. We could see the two aircraft bucking around, with the refuelling hose and basket going up and down about 20ft.'

Eventually, after some difficult flying, Biglands managed to push his probe into the refuelling basket and the fuel transfer began. But the triumph was short lived, Tuxford recalled: 'Suddenly Steve called on the radio and said "I've broken my probe!" That left us in a rather awkward position.'

With his probe broken, Biglands could take on no more fuel. The only alternative open, if the mission was to continue, was for Tuxford and Biglands to exchange roles: for Tuxford to move in behind Biglands and take back the fuel he had just given, plus sufficient take the Vulcan to Port Stanley. Now it was Bob Tuxford's task to try to take fuel from the aircraft bobbing up and down in front of him. 'I went in behind Steve's hose and had just as much difficulty as he did, trying to get in. I finally managed to make contact with a very unstable hose, and took about half of the fuel. Then the hose started to whip about and I lost contact. It took three or four minutes to make contact a second time, and just as that point we broke into clear skies, with the stars shining and no turbulence'.

From then on the fuel transfer was more or less straightforward, except that at the end of it Tuxford had somewhat less fuel than he had planned. The turbulence, and the need for the two aircraft to change places, had taken the second-to-last Victor tanker well south of the point where it should have turned back. Now it needed more fuel to complete its flight. This, coupled with the broken probe which precluded him from taking on more fuel, meant that Steve Biglands needed to retain a reasonable reserve to get back to Ascension.

As Biglands pulled his Victor round and headed north, there remained a possible legacy of the broken probe incident that could threaten the continuation of the mission. If the end of the broken refuelling probe was jammed in Tuxford's refuelling basket, the Vulcan could not take on any more fuel either. To find out, Martin Withers moved into close formation on the refuelling

basket, to allow Flight Lieutenant Dick Russell in the co-pilot's seat to inspect the basket using a hand torch. In the half-light the basket seemed all right, but the only way to be certain was for Withers to push his probe into the basket and take on a little fuel to prove the system. He did, and it was functioning perfectly.

Now the final pair of aircraft were more than 3,000 miles south of Ascension, with the Vulcan about an hour's flying time from the target. The two aircraft linked up for the final transfer of fuel before the target, at a point about 350 miles north east of Port Stanley. That transfer went ahead normally until, with the Vulcan's tanks containing about 6,000lb of fuel less than planned, Martin Withers was disconcerted to see the red indicator lights on the underside of the Victor flash on. That was the signal that the fuel transfer was complete. Withers broke radio silence with a brief request for more fuel, but Tuxford told him curtly that there could be no more. Later the Victor captain commented: 'Not being familiar with the tanking game, not knowing how far I had stretched myself to put him where he was, all he knew was that he wanted a certain amount of fuel. If only he had realised how much discussion had already taken place in my aeroplane, about how far we could afford to stretch ourselves to get him there ...'

The Victor peeled away and headed north. Unless it could take on more fuel on the way back, the tanker crew faced an invidious choice: either ditch the aircraft in the sea, or declare a full emergency and divert to an airfield in Brazil where a friendly reception could not be guaranteed. And, because of the overriding need to maintain radio silence until the Vulcan had delivered its attack, Tuxford could not communicate his predicament to those in any position to assist him.

Final preparations for attack

Although the Vulcan was also short of fuel, Martin Withers was secure in the knowing that one Victor tanker, plus a reserve, were programmed to meet him on his return flight to replenish his tanks. Now he put the problems of the previous hours behind him and made final preparations to deliver the attack. Dick Russell, attached to the crew as a flight refuelling

expert, climbed out of the co-pilot's seat and
Flying Officer Peter Taylor, who normally flew
with Withers, climbed in. At a point 290 miles to
the north of the target Withers eased back on
throttles; the bomber dropped its nose to maintain
speed and began a long descent to low altitude,
to keep it beneath the cover of any radar sets
the Argentines might have brought to the island.
Falling at about 2,000ft per minute, the Vulcan
continued on towards its target, covering a further
57 miles before it levelled out at 2,000ft. At that
point Flight Lieutenant Bob Wright, the radar
operator, switched on his equipment and made a
few sweeps of the area ahead of the bomber.

Shortly after 04.00hrs Port Stanley Time, and
46 miles from the target, it was time for Withers
to show his hand. He pushed forward the throttle
levers and the four Olympus engines wound up
to their maximum thrust. The bomber entered a
steep climb then, when he reached 10,000ft, he
levelled out for the bombing run letting his speed
build up to 400mph. When he reached that
speed he eased back on the throttles, to avoid
exceeding the maximum permissible speed at
that altitude. Meanwhile, Bob Wright had turned
on his radar again, and now he controlled the
aircraft during its bombing run.

Martin Withers could see nothing of the
target, he had merely to follow the left-right
steering signals generated by the bomber's
attack computer. Later he recalled: 'It was
a smooth night, everything was steady, the
steering signals were steady, and the range was
coming down nicely. All of the switching had
been made and 10 miles from the target we
opened the bomb doors. I was expecting flak
and perhaps missiles to come up but nothing
happened. The Air Electronics Officer didn't say
anything about the defences and I didn't ask
– I left that side of things entirely to him. I was
concentrating entirely on flying the aircraft.'

In fact a few Argentine defenders had
observed the approaching intruder on radar, and
were preparing to engage it. Flight Lieutenant
Hugh Prior, the AEO, picked up signals from
an enemy gun-control radar trying to lock on to
the bomber. Prior switched on the appropriate
jammer and the enemy signals ceased.

The Vulcan flew across the runway at an
angle of 30 degrees, and released its twenty-
one 1,000lb bombs in a long line. Given the

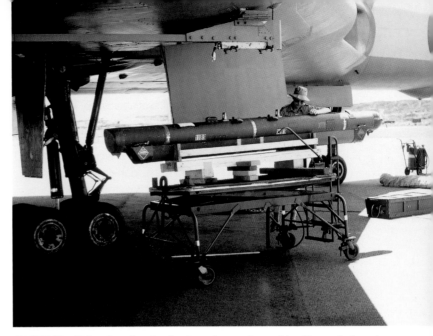

ABOVE The Vulcan's suite of noise jamming equipment had been designed
to counter Soviet Bloc air defence radars. However, those used by the
Argentine forces on the Falklands had been purchased from Western
sources. To combat the latter the Vulcan was fitted with an ALQ-101
jamming pod removed from a Buccaneer strike aircraft.

BELOW Port Stanley airfield photographed after the first two attacks by
Vulcans. The initial bomb from Martin Withers' attack hit near the middle
of the runway and cut a swathe of destruction running south west from
there. The bombs from the second 'Black Buck' attack narrowly missed the
western edge of the runway.

plane's elderly attack system, that method gave the best chance of scoring a single hit on the runway. (While an attack down the length of the runway might have produced more than one hit, even a slight error in line would have caused all the bombs to miss). In the event the first bomb to be released impacted almost exactly in the middle of the runway, and blew out a large crater. The rest exploded in a line across the airfield. His primary task complete, Malcolm Withers pushed forward the throttles and hauled the bomber into a steep climbing turn to get the Vulcan clear of the defended area as soon as possible

Shopkeeper and artist Tony Chater and his wife Ann were in bed at their home in Port Stanley town, when the bombs detonated. He recalled: 'I was half awake at the time and the whole house shook. It was as though there had been an earthquake, then we heard the "boomboomboomboom" of the bombs going off, very muffled. Shortly afterwards I just made out the sound of an aircraft in the distance ... There was terrific jubilation in Stanley. From then on we really felt very confident that the British forces were going to come to our rescue.'

As the Vulcan completed its turn and was some 14 miles away from the target and climbing away rapidly, the Port Stanley gun defences came to life. Their noisy display of defiance continued for some minutes, before one by one the weapons fell silent.

Aboard the Vulcan there was none of the jubilation felt by the residents of Port Stanley. The exertions of the previous eight hours had drained the crew of all emotion. Withers continued: 'After the attack the crew was very quiet, rather sad. We had just started a shooting war. It had all been rather cold-blooded, creeping in there at 4.30 in the morning to drop bombs on the place. But we had a job to do and we thought that job worth doing.'

The crew had no way of knowing it yet, but Bob Wright's stick of bombs had cut a swathe of destruction running south-west from the centre of the airfield. His first bomb landed almost in the centre of the runway, penetrated as planned, and then detonated to cause a large crater with considerable 'heave' around the lip. The second bomb caused damage

to the southern edge of the runway. One of his later bombs landed between the airfield's only repair hangar and a Pucara attack aircraft parked nearby, causing severe damage to both. Considering the limitations of the Vulcan's bomb-aiming system, designed for use with a nuclear weapon, the attack had been as successful as could reasonably have been hoped.

Superfuse!

Now the Vulcan clawed its way back to high altitude, where each pound of fuel burned would carry the bomber twice as far as when the bomber was low down. Meanwhile, Hugh Prior prepared his post-strike signal. He had been briefed to send one of two code words: if the attack appeared to have been successful, he would send 'Superfuse'. If the attack was not successful, but the enemy had been alerted, he would call 'Rhomboid'. If the attack had to be abandoned, but the enemy had been alerted, he was to remain silent. After a short discussion the crew agreed that the attack appeared to have been successful, so Prior broadcast the Superfuse signal on his high-frequency radio. From his base at Ascension there came an immediate acknowledgement.

At the Ministry of Defence Main Building in Whitehall there was a cheer in the RAF operations room as the news was received. Air Vice-Marshal Kenneth Hayr, Assistant Chief of the Air Staff (Operations), dashed upstairs to convey the good news personally to the Chief of the Air Staff, Air Chief Marshal Sir Michael Beetham.

Those feelings of self-congratulation quickly subsided, however, for the operation was only half complete. The second, and in many ways more difficult, part of the mission was that of getting all the aircraft safely back to Ascension.

Just over four hours after the attack, the Vulcan reached its planned refuelling point off the coast of Brazil. By now it was broad daylight and the sun was high in the sky. The crew made radio contact with the approaching Victor tanker and Martin Withers caught sight of its white underbelly as it swung into position in front of him. The tanker levelled out, the refuelling hose trailing invitingly behind it.

There was still one further drama awaiting the crew of the Vulcan, however. Withers advanced slowly on the Victor and pushed his refuelling probe into the basket. Initially the precious fuel flowed smoothly into the bomber's tanks. But then, as the pressure built up, fuel began to spill from the connection. The translucent liquid gushed over the plane's windscreen, and even with wipers running at high speed the pilots could make out only the blurred outline of the aircraft in front.

If it had been a training sortie the Vulcan pilot would have broken contact, then moved forward again to re-insert the probe into the refuelling basket. But there was a chance that the refuelling probe or the basket had suffered

damage. Withers felt that if he broke contact now, he could not be certain of regaining it. And although some fuel was being lost, most of it was flowing into the bomber's tanks. For each minute that Withers maintained the precarious contact, his bomber collected another ton of fuel.

Help then came from an unexpected quarter. Bob Wright, the Vulcan's radar operator, was standing on the ladder between the pilots' seats watching the operation. As the fuel gushed over the canopy he noticed that at the base of the centre windscreen, almost level with his eyes, the airflow kept a narrow strip of glass clear of fuel. Through that strip he was able to see the tanker clearly, and he was able to give a running

BELOW Flt Lt Martin Withers lands Vulcan XM607 at Wideawake airfield on 1 May 1982, after being airborne for 16 hours 2 minutes to deliver his attack on the airfield at Port Stanley.

Flight refuelling the Vulcan – Martin Withers

For refuelling in flight, the Vulcan had a refuelling probe located centrally on the nose and linked into the normal refuelling lines. One feature of the Vulcan that caused a minor problem, particularly at night, was that the probe and drogue were not in the pilot's direct field of vision as he approached the basket to make contact. Otherwise the Vulcan was a nice aircraft to fly during refuelling.

It was normal to join up with a tanker to one side and slightly below, and then move into line astern. Before commencing refuelling, the fuel tank pressurisation system was switched off. Then the refuelling master switch was selected on, and the refuelling valves in each of the fourteen fuel tanks opened.

After a brief period to stabilise his aircraft behind the basket, the pilot applied a little extra power, aligning himself on the

RIGHT The view from the cockpit of a Vulcan as it edges into position to take fuel from a Victor tanker.

reference points on the underside of the tanker. As the receiver moved forward with an overtaking speed of about 5kts, its pilot waited until he heard the 'clunk' as the probe engaged in the basket. The receiver pushed the hose a few feet back towards the hose/drum unit in the tanker, until the green light illuminated on the underside of the tank to indicate that the fuel was flowing. During refuelling, the co-pilot monitored the Centre of Gravity indicator to confirm that fuel was flowing into all the tanks.

When the refuelling operation was complete, the pilot of the receiver eased back on the power and the probe disconnected from the drogue. The tank pressurisation system was then switched on and the refuelling master switch was turned off.

The advantage the Vulcan had over many other large aeroplane types was that it was very stable when joining up and in contact. Also it had abundant power to refuel at high altitude to its maximum all up weight, even with twenty-one 1,000lb bombs on board.

BELOW The flight refuelling system fitted to the Vulcan.

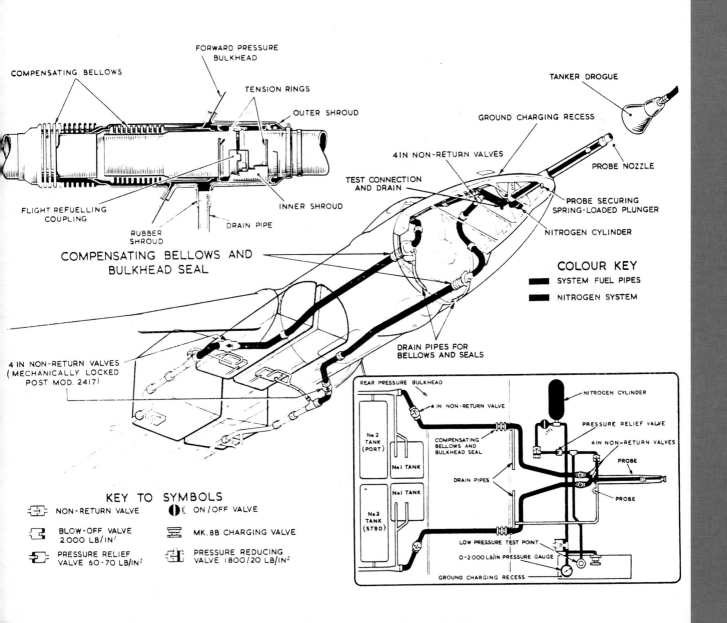

COMPENSATING BELLOWS

FORWARD PRESSURE BULKHEAD

TENSION RINGS

OUTER SHROUD

FLIGHT REFUELLING COUPLING

RUBBER SHROUD

DRAIN PIPE

INNER SHROUD

COMPENSATING BELLOWS AND BULKHEAD SEAL

TANKER DROGUE

GROUND CHARGING RECESS

4IN NON-RETURN VALVES

TEST CONNECTION AND DRAIN

PROBE NOZZLE

PROBE SECURING SPRING-LOADED PLUNGER

NITROGEN CYLINDER

COLOUR KEY

SYSTEM FUEL PIPES

NITROGEN SYSTEM

DRAIN PIPES FOR BELLOWS AND SEALS

4 IN NON-RETURN VALVES (MECHANICALLY LOCKED POST MOD. 2417)

KEY TO SYMBOLS

NON-RETURN VALVE

ON/OFF VALVE

BLOW-OFF VALVE 2000 LB/IN²

MK.8B CHARGING VALVE

PRESSURE RELIEF VALVE 60-70 LB/IN²

PRESSURE REDUCING VALVE 1800/20 LB/IN²

REAR PRESSURE BULKHEAD

No 2 TANK (PORT)

No1 TANK

No1 TANK

No 2 TANK (STBD)

4 IN NON-RETURN VALVE

NITROGEN CYLINDER

PRESSURE RELIEF VALVE

COMPENSATING BELLOWS AND BULKHEAD SEAL

4 IN NON-RETURN VALVES

DRAIN PIPES

PROBE

PROBE

LOW PRESSURE TEST POINT

0-2000 LB/IN PRESSURE GAUGE

GROUND CHARGING RECESS

RIGHT Tired and dishevelled after the long flight, Withers is pictured immediately after he climbed out of the Vulcan on 1 May.

BELOW On two of the five 'Black Buck' operations the Vulcan carried the US-made Shrike anti-radar missile, one of which is seen here fitted on the aircraft's under wing mounting.

commentary on relative positions of the two aircraft to continue the refuelling.

It took about ten minutes for the Vulcan to collect the fuel it needed. Then the bomber pulled back to break contact. A valve in the tanker shut off the supply of fuel and in an instant the airflow cleared the Vulcan's windscreen. Suddenly all was sunshine and light in the bomber, and Martin Withers felt as if a huge burden had been lifted from his shoulders: 'After that fuel was on board, the other four hours back to Ascension were a bit of a bore. Only then was the tension off and we knew we were going to make it. Those four hours seemed to last forever.'

Martin Withers and his tired crew landed at Wideawake after just over sixteen hours airborne. Bob Tuxford, having taken fuel from a Victor sent south to meet him, had landed there a couple of hours earlier.

In all seven Black Buck operations were planned, of which two had to be aborted. On three of the planned attacks the Vulcans carried the full load of twenty-one 1,000lb bombs, while during the other four missions the aircraft carried two, later four, Shrike radar-homing missiles.

What did the Vulcan Black Buck missions achieve?

That first 'Black Buck' mission had stretched the Vulcan and Victor crews almost to the limit. The effort expended in delivering the attack had been out of all proportion to the physical damage inflicted – the single bomb crater on the runway at Port Stanley and other relatively minor damage at the airfield. Yet the psychological effect of that raid on the enemy was also out of all proportion to the physical damage it had caused.

The attack had come as a complete surprise to the Argentine Military Junta, which until then had believed that the Britain's preparations for war were merely part of some elaborate bluff. The attack by the single Vulcan made it clear that the British Task Force was squaring up for a fight.

That first Vulcan attack also demonstrated

that the RAF had the capability to hit targets on the Argentine mainland, should it choose to do so. At that time the Argentine Air Force had only one dedicated fighter interceptor unit equipped with air-to-air missiles, Gruppo 8 with eleven French-built Mirage III fighters. Following the Vulcan attack on Port Stanley airfield, Gruppo 8 was ordered to leave Rio Gallegos in the south of Argentina, and move to Comodoro Rivadavia some 400 miles to the north. That move positioned the Mirages to protect military targets on the mainland, but it now left the Falkland Islands beyond their effective fighting range. With that move the Argentine Air Force abandoned any attempt to secure air superiority over the islands, and the Mirage IIIs played little further part in the air fighting.

Almost until the end of the conflict Gruppo 8 remained at Comodoro Rivadavia, awaiting an enemy attack that never came. Meanwhile, over the Falklands, the move presented the Royal Navy Sea Harriers with air superiority without having to fight for it. The jump jets were given free rein to hunt down the enemy fighter-bombers, which lacked the air-to-air missiles to fight off their tormentors. In the hard-fought actions that followed the Sea Harriers were always the hunters, they were never the hunted. And *that* was a prize that was certainly worth the effort expended in mounting the 'Black Buck' series of operations.

ABOVE Britain's former Prime Minister, Lady Thatcher, pictured during her visit to Bruntingthorpe on 2 November 2008. She is pictured with some of the crewmen who flew on the 'Black Buck' Vulcan missions during the Falklands Conflict. From left to right: Barry Masefield, Jim Vinales, Mick Cooper, Dick Russell, John Reeve and Martin Withers. *Vulcan to the Sky Trust*

Chapter 3

Anatomy of the Vulcan B2

The Vulcan B2 is an all-metal monoplane of delta plan form, powered by four Bristol Olympus engines. Although it had a futuristic appearance when it was first unveiled, both its structure and the materials used in its construction were conventional for that time. The aircraft normally had a crew of five. It could carry a heavy load of nuclear, thermonuclear or high explosive bombs over great distances, and at relatively high speeds and altitudes.

OPPOSITE A Vulcan B2 of No 617 Squadron undergoes final preparations at RAF Scampton before a night-time training sortie in August 1963 with a Blue Steel stand-off nuclear weapon. *IWM RAF T4136*

Cutaway drawing of the Vulcan B2. *Mike Badrocke*

1 Wing tip ILS antenna
2 Starboard navigation light
3 A.R.I. 18075 'Blue Diver' antenna, port and starboard
4 Outboard aileron
5 Inboard aileron
6 Rear spar
7 Outer wing panel rib structure
8 Front spar
9 Cambered leading edge ribs
10 Cranked leading edge
11 Leading edge corrugated inner skin panel
12 Retractable landing/ taxiing light
13 Fuel tank fire suppression bottles
14 Outer wing panel attachment rib joint
15 Honeycomb skin panelling
16 Outboard elevator
17 Inboard elevator
18 Elevator hydraulic actuators
19 No 7 starboard fuel tank, total internal capacity 9,260 Imp gal (42,096 lit)
20 No 5 starboard tank
21 Diagonal rib
22 Leading edge de-icing air duct
23 Wing stringers
24 Parallel chord wing skin panels

25 No. 6 starboard fuel tank
26 No. 4 starboard tank
27 No. 3 starboard tank
28 Main undercarriage leg strut and shock absorber
29 Eight-wheel main undercarriage bogie
30 Main wheel bay door
31 Fire suppression bottles
32 Inboard leading edge ribs
33 De-icing air supply
34 Fuel collectors and pumps
35 Main undercarriage wheel bay
36 Drag link and retraction actuator
37 Airborne Auxiliary Power Plant (AAPP)
38 Electrical equipment bay
39 Starboard engine bays
40 Rolls-Royce (Bristol) Olympus 301 engines
41 Engine bleed air ducting
42 Engine bay dividing rib
43 Fire suppression bottles
44 Jet pipes
45 Fixed trailing edge structure
46 Exhaust nozzle shrouds
47 Rear equipment bay
48 Oxygen bottles
49 Batteries
50 Rudder power control unit
51 Rear avionics equipment bay
52 ECM equipment packs
53 Avionics cooling air duct
54 'Red Steer' tail warning radar equipment
55 Aft radome

56 Twin brake parachute housing
57 Parachute door
58 Rubber rib structure
59 Rudder mass balances and seals
60 Fin de-icing air vent
61 Fin tip antenna fairing
62 Passive ECM antennae, fore and aft
63 Two-spar fin torsion box structure
64 Fin leading edge rib structure
65 Corrugated inner skin/ de-icing ducting
66 HF antenna
67 Fin de-icing air supply
68 Bomb bay rear bulkhead
69 Bomb bay roof arch frames
70 De-icing bleed air pre-cooler air intake
71 VHF antenna
72 Port Olympus 301 engines
73 Engine bay shroud ribs
74 Port jet pipe fairing
75 Electrical equipment bay
76 Chaff/flare launchers
77 'Green Satin' doppler navigational equipment bay
78 Elevator mass balance and seals
79 Elevator hydraulic actuators
80 Port inboard elevator
81 Port outboard elevator
82 Port inboard aileron
83 Aileron mass balance and seal

84 Control rods
85 Aileron power control units
86 Ventral actuator fairings
87 Port outboard aileron
88 Wing tip localiser antenna
89 Port navigation light
90 Cranked and cambered leading edge panel
91 Fuel tank fire suppression bottles

92 Outer wing panel joint rib
93 No. 7 port fuel tank
94 No. 5 port tank
95 Leading edge de-icing air duct
96 No. 6 port fuel tank
97 No. 4 port tank
98 No. 3 port tank
99 Port main undercarriage bay

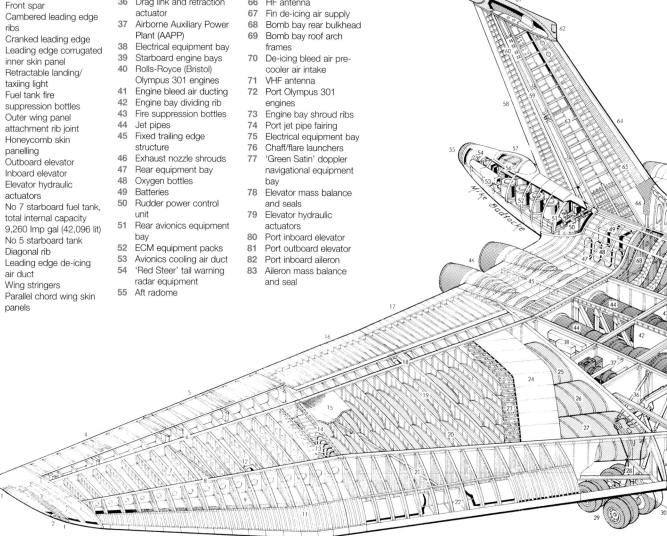

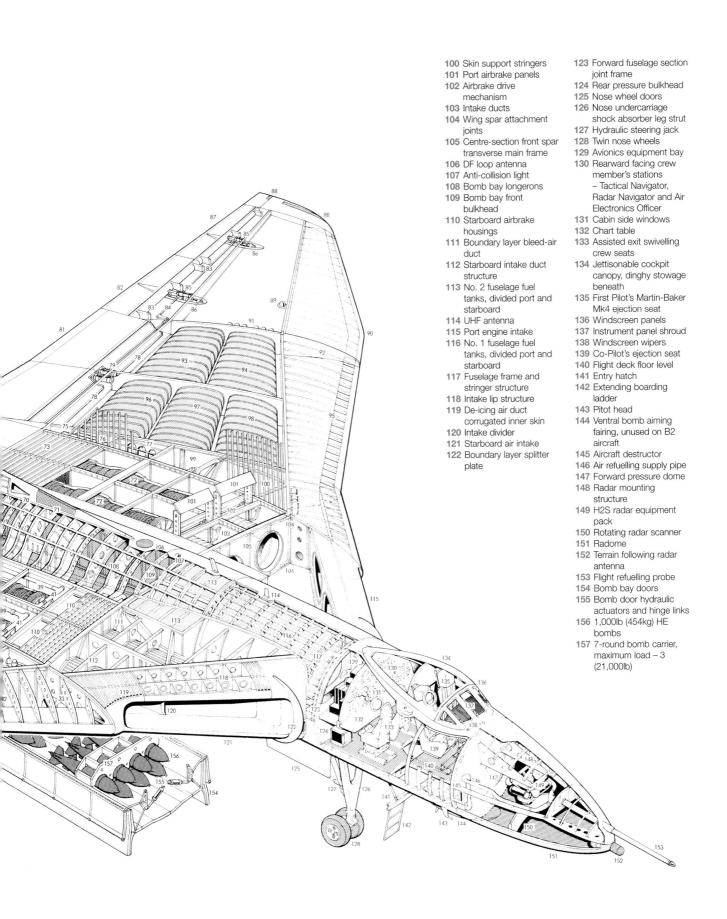

100 Skin support stringers
101 Port airbrake panels
102 Airbrake drive mechanism
103 Intake ducts
104 Wing spar attachment joints
105 Centre-section front spar transverse main frame
106 DF loop antenna
107 Anti-collision light
108 Bomb bay longerons
109 Bomb bay front bulkhead
110 Starboard airbrake housings
111 Boundary layer bleed-air duct
112 Starboard intake duct structure
113 No. 2 fuselage fuel tanks, divided port and starboard
114 UHF antenna
115 Port engine intake
116 No. 1 fuselage fuel tanks, divided port and starboard
117 Fuselage frame and stringer structure
118 Intake lip structure
119 De-icing air duct corrugated inner skin
120 Intake divider
121 Starboard air intake
122 Boundary layer splitter plate

123 Forward fuselage section joint frame
124 Rear pressure bulkhead
125 Nose wheel doors
126 Nose undercarriage shock absorber leg strut
127 Hydraulic steering jack
128 Twin nose wheels
129 Avionics equipment bay
130 Rearward facing crew member's stations – Tactical Navigator, Radar Navigator and Air Electronics Officer
131 Cabin side windows
132 Chart table
133 Assisted exit swivelling crew seats
134 Jettisonable cockpit canopy, dinghy stowage beneath
135 First Pilot's Martin-Baker Mk4 ejection seat
136 Windscreen panels
137 Instrument panel shroud
138 Windscreen wipers
139 Co-Pilot's ejection seat
140 Flight deck floor level
141 Entry hatch
142 Extending boarding ladder
143 Pitot head
144 Ventral bomb aiming fairing, unused on B2 aircraft
145 Aircraft destructor
146 Air refuelling supply pipe
147 Forward pressure dome
148 Radar mounting structure
149 H2S radar equipment pack
150 Rotating radar scanner
151 Radome
152 Terrain following radar antenna
153 Flight refuelling probe
154 Bomb bay doors
155 Bomb door hydraulic actuators and hinge links
156 1,000lb (454kg) HE bombs
157 7-round bomb carrier, maximum load – 3 (21,000lb)

53

ABOVE A plan view of Vulcan XH558 displaying the delta wing planform to full advantage. JCB

ABOVE **Flight refuelling probe.** *Jonathan Falconer*

Airframe

The airframe is divided into three main areas: the fuselage, the mainplanes and the tail unit. The fuselage is manufactured in four separate sections: the nose, the front section, the centre section and the rear section. Each section is a stressed skin structure made of light alloy. The circular cross-section

incorporated transverse formers braced by longitudinal stringers.

The upper part of the nose section is of orthodox metal construction. It houses the flight-refuelling probe, the scanner for the H2S bombing radar with its associated pneumatic system, and a 12-gallon tank for de-icing fluid for the windscreen. Below the metal structure is a dielectric radome made of fibreglass and hycar (a lightweight first

ABOVE **A plan view of Vulcan XH558 displaying the delta wing planform to full advantage.** *JCB*

BELOW **Sections of the aircraft.**

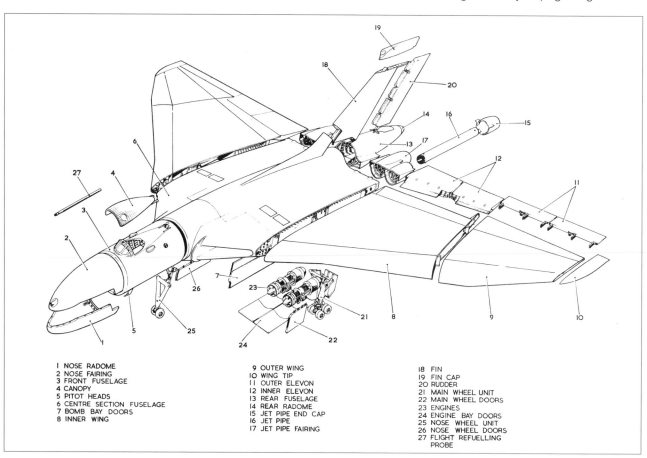

1 NOSE RADOME	9 OUTER WING	18 FIN
2 NOSE FAIRING	10 WING TIP	19 FIN CAP
3 FRONT FUSELAGE	11 OUTER ELEVON	20 RUDDER
4 CANOPY	12 INNER ELEVON	21 MAIN WHEEL UNIT
5 PITOT HEADS	13 REAR FUSELAGE	22 MAIN WHEEL DOORS
6 CENTRE SECTION FUSELAGE	14 REAR RADOME	23 ENGINES
7 BOMB BAY DOORS	15 JET PIPE END CAP	24 ENGINE BAY DOORS
8 INNER WING	16 JET PIPE	25 NOSE WHEEL UNIT
	17 JET PIPE FAIRING	26 NOSE WHEEL DOORS
		27 FLIGHT REFUELLING PROBE

generation carbon fibre that was used extensively in the manufacture of radomes).

The front section of the fuselage consists of a radome and forward and rear pressure bulkheads. The space between the bulkheads comprises the crew's pressurised cabin. The crew stations are at two levels; the two pilots, sitting on Martin Baker Mk 3K ejection seats, are positioned at the front and sit higher than the three rear crew members. The latter sit on normal-type seats facing rearwards, the Air Electronics Officer to port, the Navigator Plotter in the middle and the Navigator Radar to starboard.

On the lower surface of this section is the bomb aimer's optical sighting window, and aft of that is the main entrance and escape door. The canopy over the pilots' heads can be jettisoned, to serve as a second means of

ABOVE LEFT Front pressure bulkhead. *PRM Aviation*

ABOVE Farnborough, September 1958: co-author Tony Blackman (centre) and his crew stand beside the crew access door in the floor of the fuselage front section. *Tony Blackman*

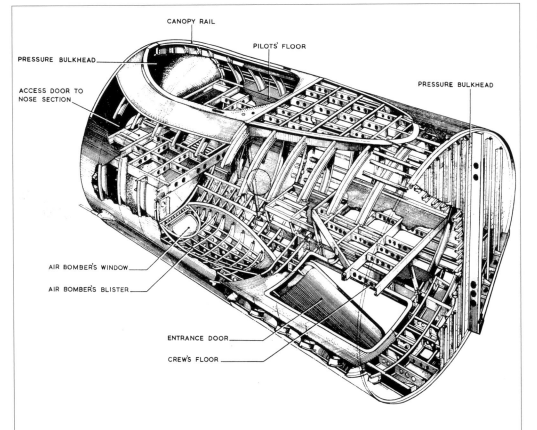

PRESSURE BULKHEAD

ACCESS DOOR TO NOSE SECTION

CANOPY RAIL

PILOTS' FLOOR

PRESSURE BULKHEAD

AIR BOMBER'S WINDOW

AIR BOMBER'S BLISTER

ENTRANCE DOOR

CREW'S FLOOR

LEFT Vulcan fuselage front section.

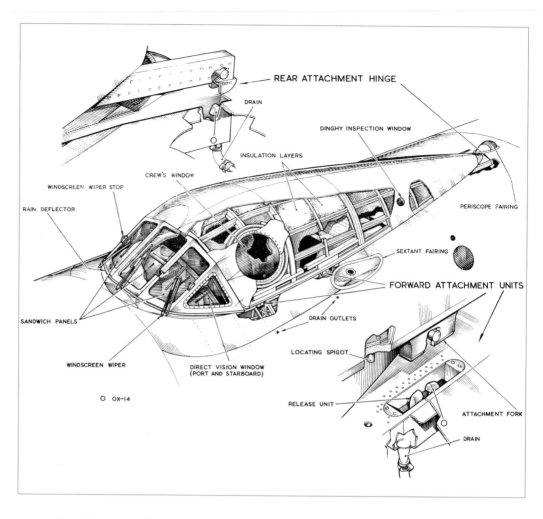

RIGHT Cockpit canopy, windscreen and associated assemblies.

REAR ATTACHMENT HINGE

DRAIN

DINGHY INSPECTION WINDOW

INSULATION LAYERS

CREW'S WINDOW

WINDSCREEN WIPER STOP

RAIN DEFLECTOR

PERISCOPE FAIRING

SEXTANT FAIRING

FORWARD ATTACHMENT UNITS

SANDWICH PANELS

DRAIN OUTLETS

LOCATING SPIGOT

WINDSCREEN WIPER

DIRECT VISION WINDOW
(PORT AND STARBOARD)

ATTACHMENT FORK

RELEASE UNIT

DRAIN

O OX-14

escape from the aircraft. The nose wheel leg attachment brackets are attached externally to the rear pressure bulkhead.

The centre section of the fuselage runs from the rear of the pressure bulkhead to a point just aft of the rear wing spar. The structure between the

rear pressure bulkhead and the front spar form the nose wheel bay, and also houses two fuel tanks.

The area between the front and the rear spars incorporates the bomb bay, which occupies the entire centre section of the aircraft. When the bomb bay doors are open, they fold

BELOW LEFT AND RIGHT The cockpit canopy is a detachable single-piece structure.

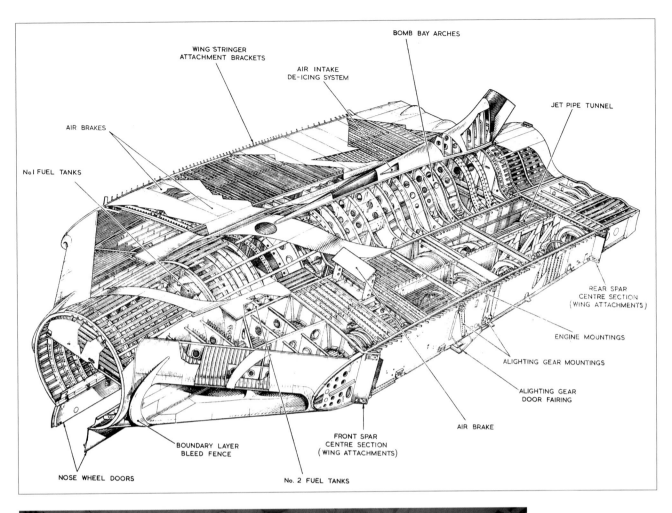

WING STRINGER
ATTACHMENT BRACKETS

BOMB BAY ARCHES

AIR INTAKE
DE-ICING SYSTEM

JET PIPE TUNNEL

AIR BRAKES

No1 FUEL TANKS

REAR SPAR
CENTRE SECTION
(WING ATTACHMENTS)

ENGINE MOUNTINGS

ALIGHTING GEAR MOUNTINGS

ALIGHTING GEAR
DOOR FAIRING

AIR BRAKE

BOUNDARY LAYER
BLEED FENCE

FRONT SPAR
CENTRE SECTION
(WING ATTACHMENTS)

NOSE WHEEL DOORS

No. 2 FUEL TANKS

ABOVE Vulcan
fuselage centre
section.

LEFT The bomb bay
interior. *Dave Morris*

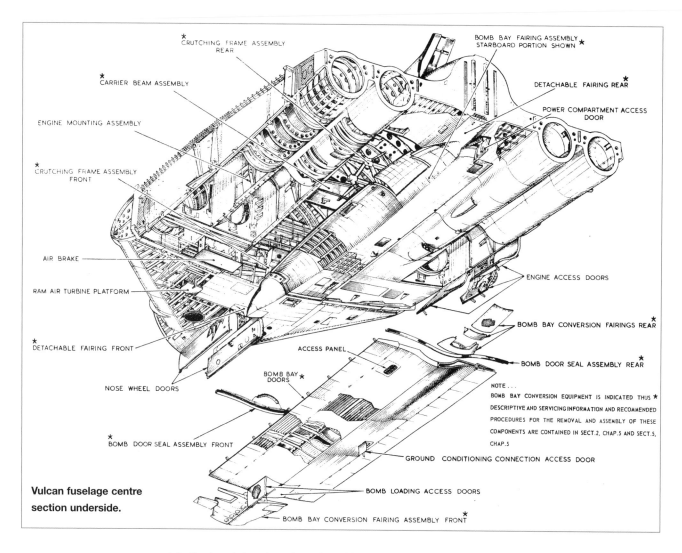

CRUTCHING FRAME ASSEMBLY
REAR

CARRIER BEAM ASSEMBLY

ENGINE MOUNTING ASSEMBLY

CRUTCHING FRAME ASSEMBLY
FRONT

AIR BRAKE

RAM AIR TURBINE PLATFORM

DETACHABLE FAIRING FRONT

NOSE WHEEL DOORS

BOMB DOOR SEAL ASSEMBLY FRONT

BOMB BAY
DOORS

ACCESS PANEL

BOMB BAY FAIRING ASSEMBLY
STARBOARD PORTION SHOWN

DETACHABLE FAIRING REAR

POWER COMPARTMENT ACCESS
DOOR

ENGINE ACCESS DOORS

BOMB BAY CONVERSION FAIRINGS REAR

BOMB DOOR SEAL ASSEMBLY REAR

NOTE . . .
BOMB BAY CONVERSION EQUIPMENT IS INDICATED THUS *
DESCRIPTIVE AND SERVICING INFORMATION AND RECOMMENDED
PROCEDURES FOR THE REMOVAL AND ASSEMBLY OF THESE
COMPONENTS ARE CONTAINED IN SECT. 2, CHAP. 5 AND SECT. 5,
CHAP. 5

GROUND CONDITIONING CONNECTION ACCESS DOOR

BOMB LOADING ACCESS DOORS

BOMB BAY CONVERSION FAIRING ASSEMBLY FRONT

**Vulcan fuselage centre
section underside.**

up into the bomb bay to reduce drag. From the
rear spar to the end of the centre section is the
electrical power compartment.

On either side of the nose wheel bay are

the engine air intakes, large 'letter box' air
inlets situated in each wing root leading edge.
The engines are located side-by-side in pairs,
two to port and two to starboard, outboard of

RIGHT Engine intakes.
Subliminal advertising
on one of the engine
blanks carries the
plaintive note 'Don't let
me die, I want to fly'.
*Vulcan to the Sky Trust/
Steve Rendle*

the bomb bay and between the front and rear spars. At the rear ends are the jet pipe tunnels.

All four engines exhaust via individual jet pipes mounted in the internal tunnels. The engine bays are fitted with turbine disc protection shields, designed to contain any turbine disc elements that fail, thereby reducing the risk of secondary failures or damage.

The rear section of the fuselage is constructed almost entirely of light alloy pressings and circular formers. This structure provides attachment points for the removable jet pipe end caps. The composite tail cone houses the brake parachute and the electronic jamming equipment.

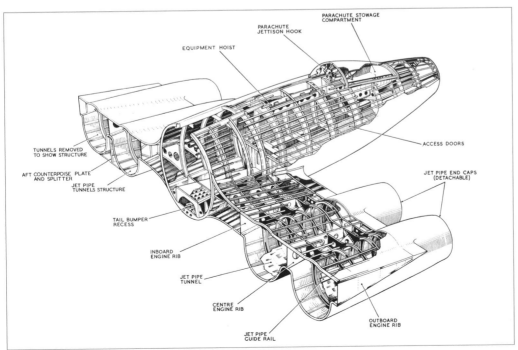

PARACHUTE STOWAGE COMPARTMENT

PARACHUTE JETTISON HOOK

EQUIPMENT HOIST

ACCESS DOORS

TUNNELS REMOVED TO SHOW STRUCTURE

AFT COUNTERPOISE PLATE AND SPLITTER

JET PIPE TUNNELS STRUCTURE

JET PIPE END CAPS (DETACHABLE)

TAIL BUMPER RECESS

INBOARD ENGINE RIB

JET PIPE TUNNEL

CENTRE ENGINE RIB

OUTBOARD ENGINE RIB

JET PIPE GUIDE RAIL

TOP LEFT AND RIGHT Rear fuselage with the engines removed, showing jet pipe tunnels and elevon attachment points. *Dave Petrie/ Vulcan to the Sky Trust*

ABOVE Jet pipe end caps. *Steve Rendle*

LEFT Vulcan fuselage rear section.

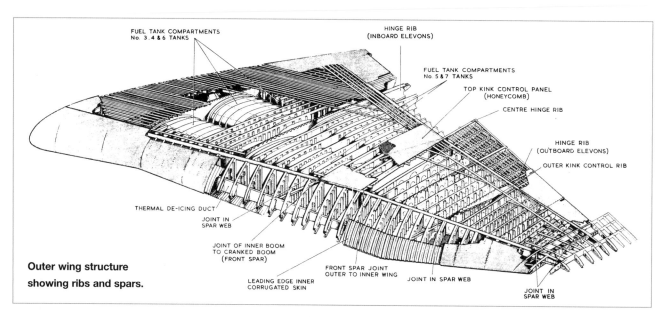

FUEL TANK COMPARTMENTS
No. 3,4 & 6 TANKS

HINGE RIB
(INBOARD ELEVONS)

FUEL TANK COMPARTMENTS
No 5 & 7 TANKS

TOP KINK CONTROL PANEL
(HONEYCOMB)

CENTRE HINGE RIB

HINGE RIB
(OUTBOARD ELEVONS)

OUTER KINK CONTROL RIB

THERMAL DE-ICING DUCT

JOINT IN
SPAR WEB

JOINT OF INNER BOOM
TO CRANKED BOOM
(FRONT SPAR)

LEADING EDGE INNER
CORRUGATED SKIN

FRONT SPAR JOINT
OUTER TO INNER WING

JOINT IN SPAR WEB

JOINT IN
SPAR WEB

**Outer wing structure
showing ribs and spars.**

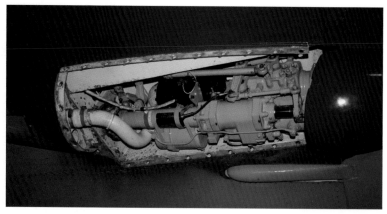

ABOVE Top view of the delta wing showing
elevons. *Jonathan Falconer*

ABOVE RIGHT Internal mechanism of PFU.
Jonathan Falconer

BELOW Wing underside showing powered flying
control units. *Jonathan Falconer*

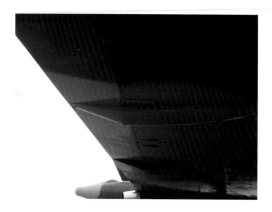

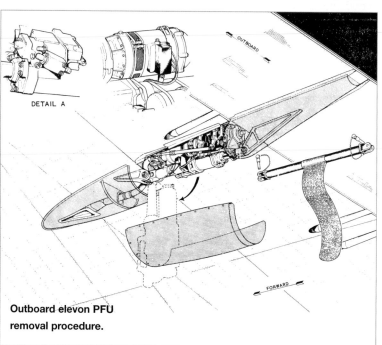

OUTBOARD

DETAIL A

FORWARD

**Outboard elevon PFU
removal procedure.**

Diagram labels:

A.A.P.P. INSTALLATION

COLD AIR INTAKES DUCTS

OLYMPUS ENGINES

THERMAL DUCTING

AIR CONDITIONING SYSTEM FEED

EXHAUST AIR EXTRACTOR

VIEW SHOWING FIN LEADING EDGE THERMAL DUCTING AND EXHAUST PORT.

EXHAUST AIR EXTRACTOR

HOT AIR VALVE

ENGINE AIR INTAKE SEPARATOR HEATER

COLD AIR INTAKE DUCTS BELOW ENGINE AIR INTAKES

LEADING EDGE DUCT

EXHAUST PORTS IN SPAR WEB

VIEW SHOWING WING LEADING EDGE THERMAL DUCTING

LEFT Thermal de-icing system installation.

BOTTOM LEFT Kinked wing leading edge. *Jonathan Falconer*

The broad delta wing layout gives the aircraft the benefit of a large wing area, without incurring the penalty of an excessive wing span. Each main plane is made up from three sections: the inner wing, the outer wing and the wing tip. They are of two-spar cantilever construction, with the inner and the outer wing sections attached by shackle joints.

To the rear of the wing structure are the attachments for the eight elevons with their powered flying control units – control surfaces on the trailing edges of the wings which operate in both the elevator and the aileron sense. At the wing leading edges there is provision for the passage of hot air for the anti-icing system.

The AAPP is buried in the fuselage behind the starboard main undercarriage leg assembly. Behind that, on each side of the aircraft, are the dispensers for chaff, rope, infra-red decoys and other defensive expendables.

The outer wing is made up from a further

Vulcan B2 – Leading Particulars

Crew:	5
Span:	111ft 0in
Length:	99ft 11in (excluding the refuelling probe)
Mainplane area:	3,965sq ft
Incidence:	5 degrees
Dihedral:	zero
Sweepback:	49 degrees 54 minutes
Fin area:	224sq ft (including the rudder)
Fin sweepback:	49 degrees 30 minutes
Height (top of fin):	27ft 1in
Track:	31ft 1in
Normal maximum all-up weight:	205,000lb
Weight empty:	99,630lb
Maximum fuel:	74,080lb (normal tankage)
Engines:	4 x Bristol Siddeley Olympus 201 turbojets each rated at 17,000lb st; or Olympus 301 turbojets each rated at 20,000lb st
Performance:	maximum level speed Mach 0.75 (528mph) at sea level, Mach 0.96 (645mph) at 39,375ft; maximum cruising speed Mach 0.95 (627mph) at 55,100ft; service ceiling 64,960ft; combat radius on internal fuel 1,710–2,300 miles; ferry range 4,750 miles, lo-lo mission 3,450 miles without refuelling; 5,750 miles with one in-flight refuelling.

Typical military loads:
- One Yellow Sun Mk 2 thermonuclear weapon, or
- One Blue Steel long range air-to-surface missile, or
- up to twenty-one 1,000lb high explosive bombs

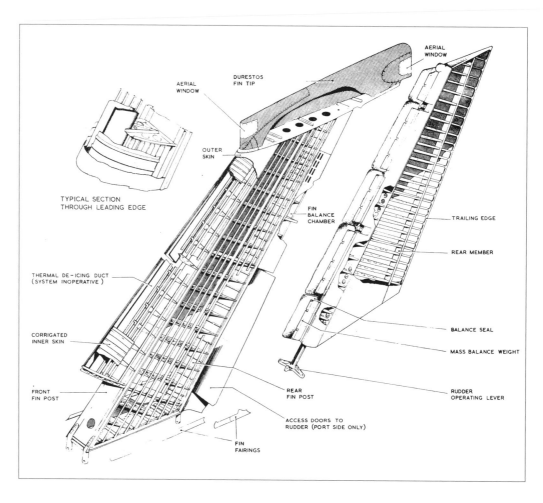

four main ribs, inter-spaced by intermediate ribs. The wing tip completes the wing structure, and provides a location for the Blue Diver ECM aerials, navigation lights and detector units.

The relatively long distance between the forward spar and the rear spar allows a thick section close to the wing root, thereby producing a very stiff structure. Each wing has a 'kinked' leading edge extension, to improve the stability of the airflow over the wing.

The tail unit comprises the dorsal fin and

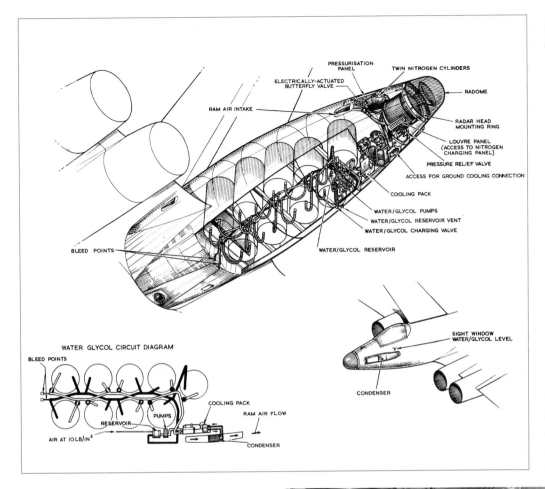

PRESSURISATION PANEL

TWIN NITROGEN CYLINDERS

ELECTRICALLY-ACTUATED BUTTERFLY VALVE

RAM AIR INTAKE

RADOME

RADAR HEAD MOUNTING RING

LOUVRE PANEL (ACCESS TO NITROGEN CHARGING PANEL)

PRESSURE RELIEF VALVE

ACCESS FOR GROUND COOLING CONNECTION

COOLING PACK

WATER/GLYCOL PUMPS

WATER/GLYCOL RESERVOIR VENT

WATER/GLYCOL CHARGING VALVE

WATER/GLYCOL RESERVOIR

BLEED POINTS

WATER GLYCOL CIRCUIT DIAGRAM

BLEED POINTS

COOLING PACK

RAM AIR FLOW

RESERVOIR

PUMPS

AIR AT 10LB/IN²

CONDENSER

SIGHT WINDOW WATER/GLYCOL LEVEL

CONDENSER

rudder, constructed from pressed ribs and skin and mounted on the rear section of the fuselage. The leading edge of the fin also has provision for hot air anti-icing. Attached at two hinge points on the trailing edge of the fin is the rudder which has two powered flying control units, a mass balance in the leading edge and its own artificial feel system. Atop the fin is a removable dielectric cap which initially housed the aerial for the Green Palm VHF jamming system but later housed an aerial for the radar warning receiver.

Olympus engines

At the time of its delivery XH558 was powered by four Bristol Siddeley Olympus 201 axial flow turbojet engines, each developing a maximum of 17,000lb of thrust. The Olympus was one of the first turbojet engines to enter production employing the so-called 'two-spool' layout. Compression takes place in two stages, with separate low pressure and high pressure

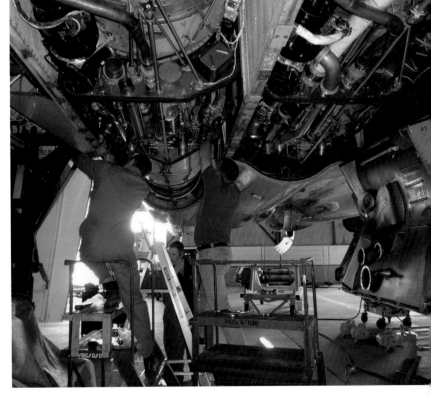

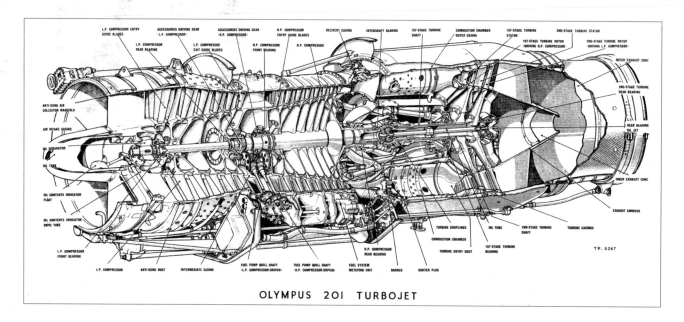

OLYMPUS 201 TURBOJET

ABOVE Cutaway of the Bristol Olympus 200 Series engine.

compressors arranged in series, each driven by its own separate turbine.

The five stage low pressure compressor is driven by the 2nd stage (rear) turbine and the seven stage high pressure compressor by the 1st stage turbine. Each compressor automatically runs at its own optimum speed, independently of the other, under all conditions of running so that high power and great efficiency can be maintained to high altitudes.

The rotor blades are mounted on seven steel discs. Between each disc is bolted a spacer ring. The entire assembly is contained between the front rotor shaft and the rear rotor centre. The front rotor shaft, which carries the compressor front bearing, the bearing seal and the driving gear, is bolted to stages No 1 and No 2. The rear rotor centre, which carries the double thrust bearing, the bearing seal, the compressor rear air seals and the compressor

RIGHT Compressor blades. *Vulcan to the Sky Trust*

FAR RIGHT Checking of the high pressure compressor blades. *Chris Collins*

RIGHT Vulcan and Concorde were both powered by the Rolls-Royce Olympus series of engines, although Concorde used the 593-series with reheat. *Jonathan Falconer collection*

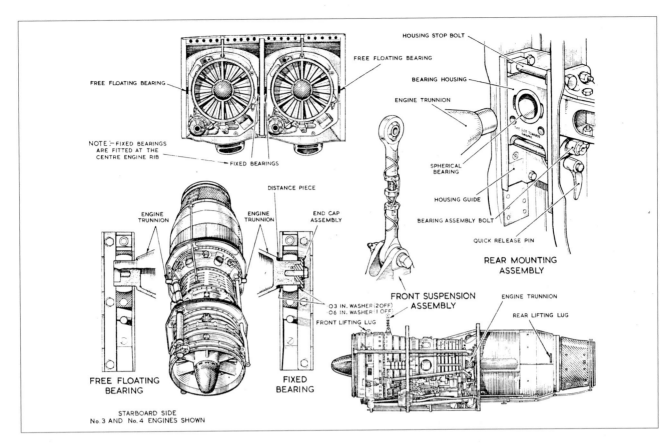

NOTE:– FIXED BEARINGS ARE FITTED AT THE CENTRE ENGINE RIB

FREE FLOATING BEARING

FREE FLOATING BEARING

FIXED BEARINGS

HOUSING STOP BOLT

FREE FLOATING BEARING

BEARING HOUSING

ENGINE TRUNNION

SPHERICAL BEARING

HOUSING GUIDE

BEARING ASSEMBLY BOLT

QUICK RELEASE PIN

REAR MOUNTING ASSEMBLY

DISTANCE PIECE

ENGINE TRUNNION

ENGINE TRUNNION

END CAP ASSEMBLY

.03 IN. WASHER (2 OFF)
.06 IN. WASHER (1 OFF)

FRONT LIFTING LUG

FRONT SUSPENSION ASSEMBLY

ENGINE TRUNNION

REAR LIFTING LUG

FREE FLOATING BEARING

FIXED BEARING

STARBOARD SIDE
No. 3 AND No. 4 ENGINES SHOWN

driving coupling, is bolted to the No 6 spacer ring and the No 7 rotor disc.

Interposed between the compressors is the intermediate casing, on which are mounted the various accessories and auxiliaries. The drives for these are taken off by spur gears on the compressor shafts. These are then transmitted, via spur and bevel gears, to the various components mounted on the outside of the casing.

Air from the high pressure compressor passes through the delivery casing, and enters the annulus formed between the turbine mounting and the combustion chamber outer casing. The eight combustion chambers are of the 'cannular' type. Each combustion chamber

ABOVE Olympus engine mounting, trunnion and suspension points.

Olympus Engine – Leading Particulars

Engine Mk	Mk 101	Mk 104	Mk 201	Mk 301
Thrust	11,000	13,000	17,000	21,000
Weight	3,615	3,857	4,149	4,070
Fuel consumption lb/hr per lb thrust	.817	.855	.837	.809
Length	127.1in	126.0in	126.5in	155.33in
Diameter	40.0in	43.5in	43.5in	44.5in
Engine RPM	6,325	6,525	6,680	6,615
Oil tank capacity	8 galls	6.5 galls	6.0	7.0
Air flow	171.5lb/sec	200lb/sec	240lb/sec	282lb/sec
Max jpt	615°	634°	670°	620°
Overall compression ratio	9.6/1	10.9/1	12.5/1	12.9/1

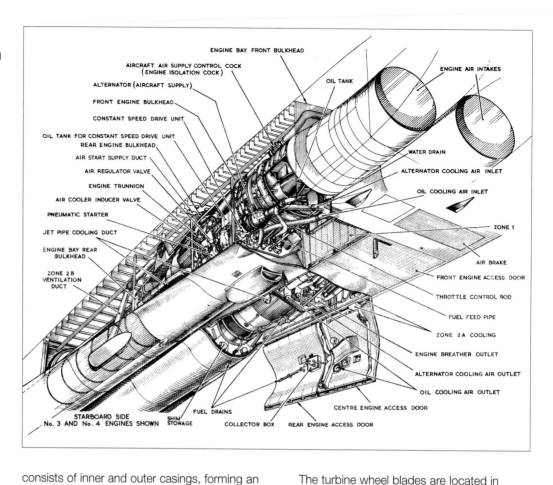

ENGINE BAY FRONT BULKHEAD

AIRCRAFT AIR SUPPLY CONTROL COCK
(ENGINE ISOLATION COCK)

ALTERNATOR (AIRCRAFT SUPPLY)

FRONT ENGINE BULKHEAD

CONSTANT SPEED DRIVE UNIT

OIL TANK FOR CONSTANT SPEED DRIVE UNIT
REAR ENGINE BULKHEAD

AIR START SUPPLY DUCT

AIR REGULATOR VALVE

ENGINE TRUNNION

AIR COOLER INDUCER VALVE

PNEUMATIC STARTER

JET PIPE COOLING DUCT

ENGINE BAY REAR
BULKHEAD

ZONE 2 B
VENTILATION
DUCT

OIL TANK

ENGINE AIR INTAKES

WATER DRAIN

ALTERNATOR COOLING AIR INLET

OIL COOLING AIR INLET

ZONE 1

AIR BRAKE

FRONT ENGINE ACCESS DOOR

THROTTLE CONTROL ROD

FUEL FEED PIPE

ZONE 2A COOLING

ENGINE BREATHER OUTLET

ALTERNATOR COOLING AIR OUTLET

OIL COOLING AIR OUTLET

STARBOARD SIDE
No. 3 AND No. 4 ENGINES SHOWN

SHIM STOWAGE

FUEL DRAINS

COLLECTOR BOX

REAR ENGINE ACCESS DOOR

CENTRE ENGINE ACCESS DOOR

BELOW AND BELOW
RIGHT **Close-ups of
the engine exhausts
and jet pipe end caps.**
Vulcan to the Sky Trust

consists of inner and outer casings, forming an
annular space which contains the flame tubes.
The combustion chambers are interconnected
by flexible metal joints, to assist flame
propagation. The Nos 4 and 6 combustion
chambers are fitted with igniter plugs, which are
used only during engine starting.

The outlet of each combustion chamber is
connected to a turbine entry duct. The rear
portion of the eight ducts forms an annulus,
which allows an even temperature distribution
and unrestricted gas flow to the turbines.

The turbine wheel blades are located in
the turbine discs by fir tree roots. These are
shrouded, to prevent gas escaping in the gap
between the blade tips and the turbine casing
and thereby reducing turbine efficiency.

Each engine is fitted with two fuel pumps.
One is driven by the low pressure compressor
rotor, the other by the high pressure
compressor rotor. Each pump consists of a
rotor supported by a cylindrical carbon bearing.
Formed inside it are seven inclined cylinders
which accommodate the steel pumping pistons.

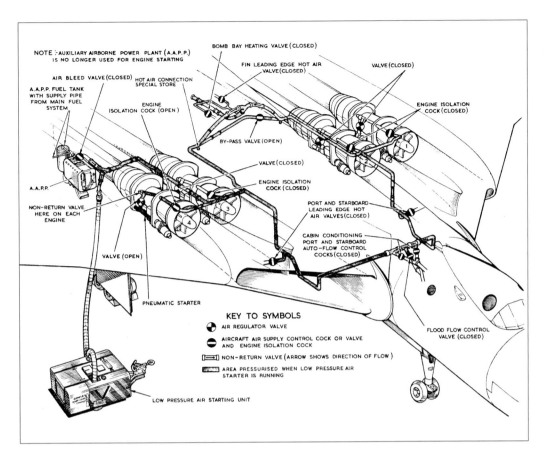

NOTE :- AUXILIARY AIRBORNE POWER PLANT (A.A.P.P.) IS NO LONGER USED FOR ENGINE STARTING

AIR BLEED VALVE (CLOSED)

BOMB BAY HEATING VALVE (CLOSED)

FIN LEADING EDGE HOT AIR VALVE (CLOSED)

VALVE (CLOSED)

A.A.P.P. FUEL TANK WITH SUPPLY PIPE FROM MAIN FUEL SYSTEM

HOT AIR CONNECTION SPECIAL STORE

ENGINE ISOLATION COCK (OPEN)

ENGINE ISOLATION COCK (CLOSED)

BY-PASS VALVE (OPEN)

VALVE (CLOSED)

ENGINE ISOLATION COCK (CLOSED)

A.A.P.P.

PORT AND STARBOARD LEADING EDGE HOT AIR VALVES (CLOSED)

NON-RETURN VALVE HERE ON EACH ENGINE

CABIN CONDITIONING PORT AND STARBOARD AUTO-FLOW CONTROL COCKS (CLOSED)

VALVE (OPEN)

PNEUMATIC STARTER

FLOOD FLOW CONTROL VALVE (CLOSED)

KEY TO SYMBOLS

AIR REGULATOR VALVE

AIRCRAFT AIR SUPPLY CONTROL COCK OR VALVE AND ENGINE ISOLATION COCK

NON-RETURN VALVE (ARROW SHOWS DIRECTION OF FLOW)

AREA PRESSURISED WHEN LOW PRESSURE AIR STARTER IS RUNNING

LOW PRESSURE AIR STARTING UNIT

The pistons are located by the auxiliary cam plate, which is mounted on a universal thrust ball on the pump drive shaft.

Engine starting – normal operation

With the engine start master switch 'ON', the ignition switch 'ON', the air selector switch set to 'NORMAL' and a ground air supply connected, air is fed through the aircraft air system up to the engine air cocks. The by-pass valve opens automatically on selection of the engine master switch 'ON'. Air is then fed to the pneumatic starter by selecting the appropriate engine air switch 'OPEN'. Pressing the individual engine start button opens the pneumatic starter air control valve.

When starting the remaining engines using air supplied by a running engine, this must be either No 1 or No 4 engine. The running engine must be set at 70 per cent revs per minute to start an individual engine, or 90 per cent revs for a simultaneous start of the three remaining engines.

Engine starting – rapid start

Early in the bomber's operational career there arose a requirement to reduce the time taken for aircraft to get airborne during a scramble take off. The new system allowed all four engines to be started simultaneously, thereby enabling a flight of four aircraft to get airborne within the specified four-minute scramble time. Five wire-bound high-pressure air storage cylinders, of 4,260 litres capacity at 3,500psi, provided compressed air to drive the starting system.

With the engine master switch 'ON', the ignition switch 'ON' and the air selector switch to 'RAPID', operation of the rapid start push-button simultaneously opened the four shut-off cocks in the air storage systems. It also energised the engine and the starter ignition circuits. Compressed air at 3,300psi is released from the high-pressure system and passed through the 3,300 to 300psi pressure-reducing valve. It enters the combustor unit, and is directed two ways. Part of the supply enters the combustion chamber, to provide cooling for the flame tubes. The remainder of the air passes through holes in the combustor unit casing, and enters the air compartment above the piston in the fuel chamber. A pressure of approximately 250psi is imparted to the piston which forces the fuel, through the retaining valve, to enter the combustor flame tube in the form of vapour.

On entry into the flame tube, the vapour ignites and the resultant high-energy gas discharge (36psi at 1,000 degrees C) into the starter turbine, is sufficient to bring the engine up to idling speed in about 20 seconds. Then a centrifugal trip switch causes the shut-off cocks to close, and the combustor ignition circuit is isolated. The resultant loss of pressure in the air compartment of the fuel chamber allows the piston to rise, the fuel-retaining valve to close and the engine to wind up. The four main alternators then come on line automatically, the powered flying control units run up to speed and the aircraft is ready to move off.

Today multi-spool turbojet and turbofan engines, and cannular combustion systems, are commonplace, but in the late 1950s these concepts represented cutting-edge technology. Early in the service life of the Vulcan B2, the Olympus 301 engine replaced the 201 in service. By fitting an extra stage to the low pressure compressor and another to the low pressure turbine, the maximum thrust of the engine was increased to 21,000lb. Due to the increase in the mass of air passing through the new engine, the Vulcan's air intakes had to be widened. At the same time, the extra stages fitted to the compressor and the turbine meant that the new engine was somewhat longer than its predecessor, and therefore the Vulcan's engine bays had to be enlarged to accommodate the later engine.

Electrical system

The Vulcan B2's main electrical system runs at 200 Volts 400 cycles three-phase alternating current, produced by the aircraft's four 40kVA engine-driven alternators. The alternating current (AC) system produces higher power levels at greater efficiency and higher reliability, than the direct current (DC) system fitted to the Vulcan B1.

To give an AC system flexibility, there needs to be provision for the each alternator to work in parallel with one or more of the others, to share the loads. However, alternators running in parallel need to produce outputs with the same output frequency, to within fine limits. So each engine-driven alternator needs to maintain a constant output frequency and maintain it over a wide range of engine speeds. To achieve this result, a constant speed drive unit (CSDU) is installed between each engine and its alternator. The CSDUs produce a constant rotational output of 6,000rpm, from any input rotational speed between 3,000rpm and 8,100rpm. That equates to an alternating current of 400 cycles. Lower voltages, required by some items of equipment, are generated from the main supply by transformer rectifier units

Since the Vulcan B2 has no reversionary manual back-up system for the flying controls, it is necessary for the system to have separate back-up electrical generation systems in case of a multiple failure. For that reason the aircraft carries a Rover AAPP fitted with an additional 40kVA alternator. There is also a wind driven ram air turbine (RAT) with a 17kVA alternator. The RAT generates its full power at 250kts (indicated) at altitudes above 20,000ft. The unit is released into the slipstream by pulling a toggle above the pilots' instrument panel. Thus, even in the event of a major electrical failure of the main alternators, there is enough redundancy in the system to ensure there is sufficient electrical power to drive the aircraft's essential systems.

To ensure that supplies are available to all consumer loads in the event of severe damage, for example due to enemy action, some main supply feeders are duplicated, others triplicated and some even quadruplicated.

As well as having redundant systems for generating electrical power, there is also a system to shed non-priority electrical loads rapidly in the event of an electrical emergency. The electrical loads are divided into three major groups: non-essential, essential and vital. Non-essential electrical systems are those systems that use large amounts of electrical power but which are not, strictly speaking, necessary to maintain the aircraft in the air. Typical among these are the bombing and other radars and the electronic countermeasures systems (with the exception of the defensive expendable systems). Pulling the RAT toggle releases the wind driven turbine into the airflow, and it begins generating electrical power immediately. At the same time, power is withdrawn from the non-essential loads and these shut down automatically.

The aircraft continues to fly, with electrical power going to priority items such as the powered flying control units, the fuel pumps, basic instruments, etc. If there is a rapid deceleration – for example in the event of a crash landing – inertia switches cut off the electrical power from all systems except for those designated as vital, namely the various fire extinguishing systems, which are then activated.

Powered Flying Controls (PFCs)

Due to the heavy aerodynamic loading on the control surfaces in large high speed aircraft, it is not practicable for a pilot to move

the control surfaces manually. In the Vulcan, the control surfaces are moved by hydraulic pressure obtained from pumps driven by electric motors. In all, there are nine control surfaces and ten electro-hydraulic powered flying control (PFC) units. Each wing has four surfaces each with its own separate unit. The rudder has two PFC units.

The pilots' control columns and rudder pedals are connected to the power units by conventional control runs. In the PFC units, the control runs move only small valves which direct the oil pressure to one side or other of a hydraulic ram. The ram then moves the control surface.

On the Vulcan B2, the conventional aileron and elevator surfaces are combined to form a system of control surfaces known as elevons, four on the trailing edge of each wing. If the pilot operates the control column to achieve climb or descent, only, the elevons all work as elevators. If he operates the control column

BELOW Flying controls mechanism.

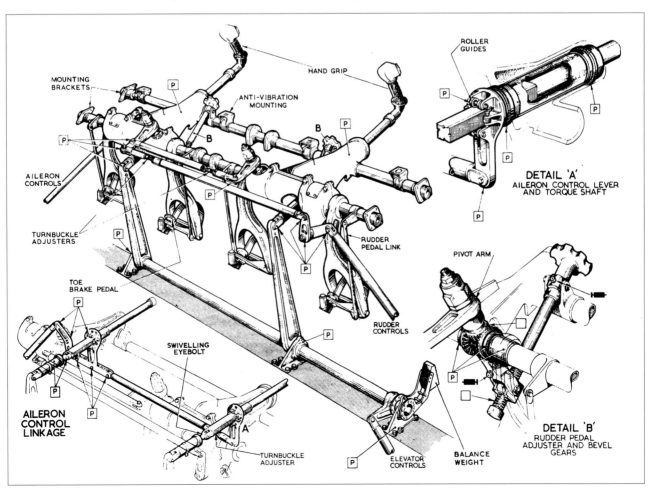

ABOVE **Air brakes deployed.** *Damien Burke*

elevon or rudder, the greater the compression required. The mechanical advantage between the control run and the spring varies with airspeed: the faster the aircraft flies, the greater the effort required to achieve a given surface movement.

The aileron sense feel unit works differently, in that feel is provided by the effort required to twist two torsion bars. This effort is constant, whatever the airspeed. The amount of control surface movement available to execute banking manoeuvres is progressively reduced as the airspeed increases. Should a malfunction occur in any of the artificial feel systems, the failed system can be switched off.

By making control column selections move the control surfaces during flight, the pilot can trim the aircraft as required but he would need to apply force continually to the control column, to keep the aircraft in trim. An electrical trimmer actuator is fitted in the input connect to each artificial feel unit and by controlling its extension or retraction, the pilot can allow the feel springs or the torsion bars to return to their neutral positions. By removing the load on the control column while leaving the trimming selection on the control surfaces, the control column and the control surfaces do not move as the trimmer actuator moves. An emergency system is provided so that, should the normal system fail, trimming facilities are still available.

to achieve bank, only, all the elevons work as ailerons. The system thus provides not only very effective aerodynamic control, but it also provides continuing control of the aircraft even if a failure affects one or more of the eight pumping units.

The rudder has only a single control surface, and duplication of drive is provided by having two power units. Normally both rudder PFC units run together, and both receive signals from the rudder pedals. But only the main (starboard) PFC unit moves the rudder surface, while the other PFC unit idles. If the main unit fails, the rudder auxiliary unit takes over automatically.

Artificial feel

With a basic system of powered flying controls, the only resistance to the movement of the control surfaces lies in the friction in the control runs. Only a small effort is required to move the servo valves in the PFC units, so with the basic system the pilot is denied the feel of flying a normally controlled aircraft. To compensate for this, the aircraft has artificial feel systems, to make the effort required to execute a given manoeuvre dependant on the airspeed and on the amount of control movement involved.

The method of achieving artificial feel in both the elevator and the rudder controls is similar. Each of their control runs is connected to a spring which is compressed each time a control run is moved. The larger the movement of the

Air brakes

The three-position rotating flap air brakes are mounted between the main ribs of the engine compartment, aft of the front spar. They are of the slat type, electrically operated. Power comes from two electric motors running off the aircraft's main electrical system. There are two sets of air brakes, one on the port side and one on the starboard side. Both sets are mounted on the centre section of the fuselage, above and below the engine air intakes. Each set of air brakes consists of two slats above the centre section and one slat below it. The upper and the lower pairs of air brakes, when extended or retracted, move in opposition to each other on spool type rollers. They are attached to the main structural ribs on either side of the engine air intake tunnels.

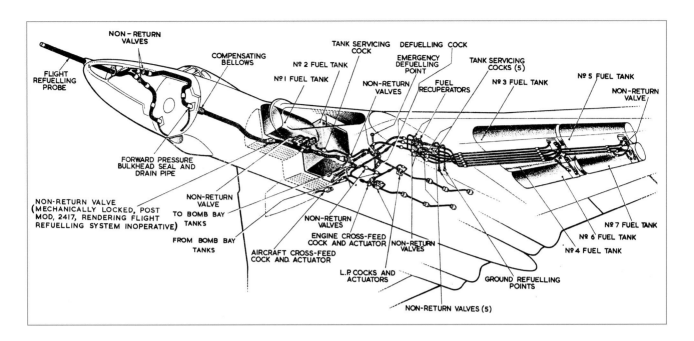

NON-RETURN VALVES
COMPENSATING BELLOWS
Nº 2 FUEL TANK
Nº 1 FUEL TANK
TANK SERVICING COCK
DEFUELLING COCK
EMERGENCY DEFUELLING POINT
TANK SERVICING COCKS (5)
Nº 3 FUEL TANK
Nº 5 FUEL TANK
FLIGHT REFUELLING PROBE
NON-RETURN VALVES
FUEL RECUPERATORS
NON-RETURN VALVE
FORWARD PRESSURE BULKHEAD SEAL AND DRAIN PIPE
NON-RETURN VALVE (MECHANICALLY LOCKED, POST MOD. 2417, RENDERING FLIGHT REFUELLING SYSTEM INOPERATIVE)
NON-RETURN VALVE TO BOMB BAY TANKS
FROM BOMB BAY TANKS
AIRCRAFT CROSS-FEED COCK AND ACTUATOR
NON-RETURN VALVES
ENGINE CROSS-FEED COCK AND ACTUATOR
NON-RETURN VALVES
L.P. COCKS AND ACTUATORS
NON-RETURN VALVES (5)
GROUND REFUELLING POINTS
Nº 7 FUEL TANK
Nº 6 FUEL TANK
Nº 4 FUEL TANK

Fuel system

The two No 1 and two No 2 fuel tanks are housed in the centre section of the fuselage, aft of the pressure bulkhead. The remaining ten fuel tanks are housed, five in each wing, between the first main rib and the second main rib. There are nine intermediate ribs, each with three apertures, and these are the locations for fuel tank bays Nos 3, 4 and 6. Between the second main rib and the third main rib there are a further nine intermediate ribs, and these house the Nos 5 and 7 tanks.

These fuel tank bays are lined with light alloy

ABOVE Fuel system installation.

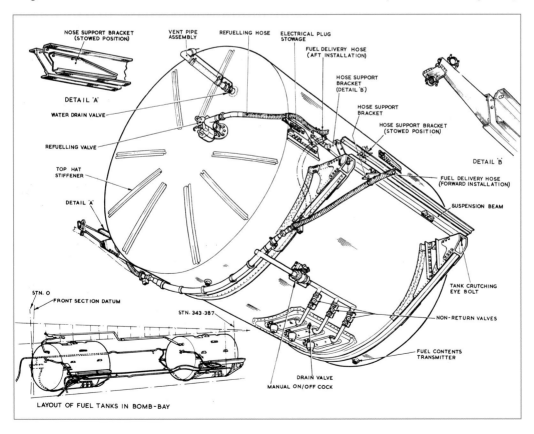

NOSE SUPPORT BRACKET (STOWED POSITION)
VENT PIPE ASSEMBLY
REFUELLING HOSE
ELECTRICAL PLUG STOWAGE
FUEL DELIVERY HOSE (AFT INSTALLATION)
HOSE SUPPORT BRACKET (DETAIL 'B')
DETAIL 'A'
WATER DRAIN VALVE
HOSE SUPPORT BRACKET
HOSE SUPPORT BRACKET (STOWED POSITION)
DETAIL 'B'
REFUELLING VALVE
TOP HAT STIFFENER
FUEL DELIVERY HOSE (FORWARD INSTALLATION)
DETAIL 'A'
SUSPENSION BEAM
TANK CRUTCHING EYE BOLT
STN. 0
FRONT SECTION DATUM
STN. 343·387
NON-RETURN VALVES
FUEL CONTENTS TRANSMITTER
DRAIN VALVE
MANUAL ON/OFF COCK
LAYOUT OF FUEL TANKS IN BOMB-BAY

LEFT Bomb bay cylindrical tank.

RIGHT Bomb
bay saddle tanks
installation.

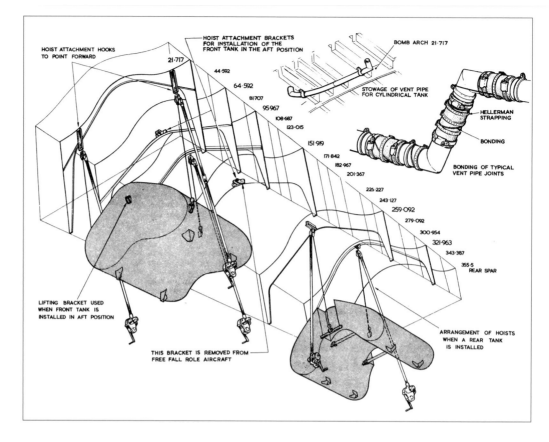

BELOW Six Vulcan
bombers were
converted to the air-
to-air refuelling role
in 1982, prior to the
introduction of the
VC10 tankers. This is
XM571, one of the K2
conversions flown by
50 Squadron.

sheet, to provide support for the collapsible
bag-type fuel tanks. Due to the reduced
depth caused by the taper of the mainplane
in both plan and elevation, the Nos 5, 6 and

7 fuel tank ribs are supported by tie rods
passed up from the underside of the main
plane. Outboard of the third main rib are six fire
extinguisher bottles.

Landing gear

The landing gear comprises two main wheel units which retract forwards and upwards into each main plane, and a nose wheel unit that retracts rearwards into the fuselage aft of the pressure cabin.

Each main wheel unit comprises a four-wheeled, eight-tyred bogie, which allows the Vulcan to operate from relatively low-strength (LCN) runways. The nose wheel has two wheels on a common axle, and is hydraulically steered.

When the main wheel units are fully extended, they are secured in the down position by hydraulically operated down-lock jacks. The nose wheel is locked in the down position by a latch lock, operated when the retraction jack reaches the fully extended position.

When the main wheel units are retracted, the bogies are 'trimmed' so they fit into the wheel bay provided for them in each main plane. The main wheel units are enclosed in their bays by a single fairing door, which is opened and

LEFT Main gear leg and wheel bogie.

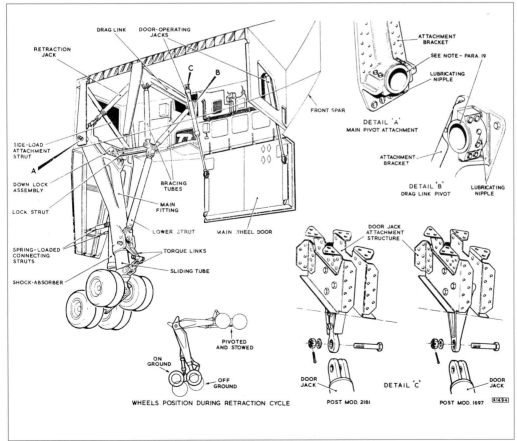

LEFT Main undercarriage assemblies.

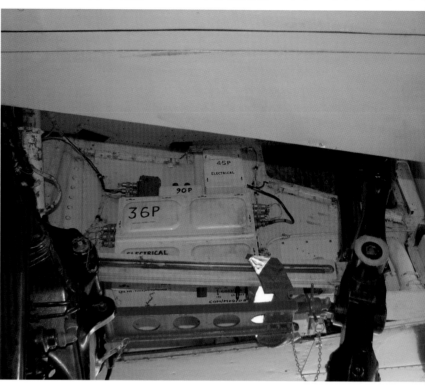

ABOVE The robust
undercarriage door
latch. *Steve Rendle*

ABOVE RIGHT
Inside the main
undercarriage bay.
Steve Rendle

RIGHT Line-up of
Vulcan B2s at RAF
Scampton in June
1963. *Jonathan Falconer
collection*

closed by two hydraulic jacks. The nose wheel bay is enclosed by two fairing doors. The wheels are raised and lowered and the doors opened and closed also by hydraulic jacks. The undercarriage units have no up locks, and are held in place by hydraulic pressure. The doors are strongly constructed, so that if the hydraulic pressure fails the doors will carry the weight of the units.

If the hydraulic system fails, the undercarriage can be lowered by pulling the emergency control handle located on the starboard side of the throttle pedestal. Two separate air supplies, contained in cylinders in the nose wheel bay, are directed to the undercarriage door jacks and wheel jacks, to open the doors and lower the undercarriage.

Airborne Auxiliary Power Plant (AAPP)

The Airborne Auxiliary Power Plant (AAPP) comprises a Rover gas turbine driving a 40 kVA alternator. It is enclosed in a stainless steel box, mounted in a bay immediately aft of the starboard main undercarriage leg. The AAPP has two main operational functions. Firstly, it provides an in-flight emergency source of 200 volt 400Hz three-phase electrical supply at altitudes below 30,000ft. Secondly, it provides electrical power for ground servicing, thereby allowing the aircraft to operate independent of supporting services when away from base. The AAPP is controlled from the AEO's position.

The engine has a centrifugal compressor, driven by a single stage axial turbine mounted on a common shaft. Air is admitted via a scoop at the underside of the AAPP bay and ducted to the compressor stage. The compressed air then passes to a single, reverse-flow, combustion chamber where it is mixed with fuel and ignited. The resultant high energy gases are directed against the blades of the turbine

RIGHT **Nose wheel main leg steering jack.**
Jonathan Falconer

by a fixed nozzle ring assembly and are then exhausted to atmosphere via a circular opening aft of the scoop.

Bomb bay doors

The bomb bay doors enclose the bomb bay, which runs the full length of the centre section between the front and rear spars. The doors are each made of two sections hinged along their length and hydraulically operated. They fold along their length about centrally disposed intermediate hinges. The halves of each door are constructed from two long beam members, made from plate web and extruded sections. Hinged doors are fitted at the forward end of the inner bomb doors, to allow access to the bomb bay for servicing without the need to open the bomb bay doors themselves.

The doors are actuated by pairs of hydraulic jacks placed at the front and rear of the bomb bay. Via a lever arm bell crank and adjustable links, the jacks fold and unfold the doors for opening or closing. There are also telescopic struts evenly spaced in the mid-length of the doors, two per side, which act as damping devices to limit any tendency for the centre section of the doors to move in flight.

The switches at the pilots' station are as follows:

■ Normal Selector Switch – this is a three-position rotary switch marked, 'OPEN – AUTO – CLOSED'. The open and closed positions are for normal selection, whilst the auto position ensures the automatic opening of the doors as a part of the bombing operation. After bomb release, the doors are closed using the normal selector switch.

■ Emergency Jettison Switch – this switch is a double pole type marked, 'JETTISON' and 'OVERRIDE'. When operated to the jettison position, this switch causes the bomb doors to open, cutting the supply to bomb fusing units. When the doors are fully open the bombs are released and then, in conjunction with a time delay, the doors are closed. The override position cancels the jettison circuit input, if the pilot changes his mind.

■ Emergency Selection Switch – a double pole switch marked 'OPEN', 'NORMAL' and 'CLOSED'. This is used if there is a failure of the normal system. The 'OPEN' and 'CLOSED' positions start the hydraulic power pack motor, energise the emergency selector and the by-pass valve, and cut off the electric supply to the normal selectors. The normal position completes the circuit of the normal system and cuts off the emergency opening and closing electrical supply.

Navigators' Bomb Door Selector – a single pole-type switch marked, 'CLOSED' and 'OPEN', it operates the bomb doors through the normal hydraulic selectors. The three-position magnetic indicator gives the following condition indications:

BELOW Bomb bay doors. *Vulcan to the Sky Trust*

BELOW RIGHT Bomb bay doors open. *Damien Burke*

- Black = doors closed
- Black and White = doors travelling (not open or closed)
- White = doors fully open

Brake parachute

The aircraft is fitted with a GQ (Irvin GQ Parachute, now known as Airborne Systems) ribbon-type brake parachute system, to provide additional aerodynamic braking should this be required after landing. The parachute is stowed in a compartment just aft of the fin, and is released when a pilot operates a switch on the centre panel labelled 'TAIL PARA – STREAM/JETTISON'. When 'STREAM' is selected, the spring loaded door to the parachute compartment pops open and the extractor parachute, 8½ft in diameter, is ejected into the airflow. The extractor then withdraws the main parachute, 45ft in diameter and of the ring slot type, out of its containing bag and assists it to deploy. When the pilot has obtained the extra braking required, he operates the same switch to jettison the parachute.

Pneumatic system

The pneumatic systems fitted to the aircraft are of two types: 'stored' and 'engine compressor air'. The stored types are operated from ground charged storage bottles and are as follows:

- Emergency lowering of the undercarriage.
- Hydraulic reservoir and power pack pressurisation.
- Entrance door closing, seal inflation and canopy seal inflation.
- Bomb aimer's windscreen de-icing system pressurisation.
- Entrance door emergency opening and canopy jettison.
- Engine Rapid Start.

Secondary systems operated from engine air supplies comprise:

- The engine air system.
- Anti-icing system.
- Fuel tank pressurisation and recuperator air pressure.
- Bomb bay door seal inflation.

ABOVE Brake parachute and air brakes fully deployed.
Vulcan to the Sky Trust

Chapter 4

The Pilot's View

Tony Blackman

Tony Blackman trained in the RAF as a test pilot, then joined Avro in 1956 just before the first Vulcan B1 was delivered to the Service. He helped to develop later versions of the Vulcan B1 and the B2, and became Chief Test Pilot in 1970. Altogether he flew 105 of the 135 Vulcans built, and amassed a total of 1,272 hours in the course of 850 flights. He tested XH558 in June 1960 and delivered it to RAF Waddington on 1 July 1960.

He also flew XH558 when it returned to Woodford for the Skybolt strengthening modifications in 1965. The account that follows concentrates mainly on his time with the Vulcan B2

OPPOSITE Vulcan B1 and its crew of No 230 OCU at RAF Waddington. *IWM RAF T1206*

ABOVE Access to the
Vulcan cockpit was
through a downward
hinging hatch on the
underside of the nose
section. *Credit?*

**ABOVE Access to the
Vulcan cockpit was
through a downward
hinging hatch on the
underside of the nose
section.** *Credit?*

**BELOW Co-author
Tony Blackman (left).**
Tony Blackman

M y introduction to the Vulcan was at
RAF Boscombe Down in 1956 when,
as a flight lieutenant test pilot, I served on the
acceptance team which checked that the
aircraft delivered from the manufacturer met
the RAF's handling requirements. We also had
to measure the performance capability of each
aircraft, to see it met the design requirements
as a weapon of war. Four months later my role
as a test pilot changed. I left the RAF and joined
the team at Avro developing improved versions
of the Vulcan B1, and the new Vulcan B2.

I also had the routine task of testing production
aircraft prior to delivery to the RAF.

The first thing one noticed when preparing
to fly the Vulcan, was the thickness of the
book of checklists. Known previously as *Pilots'
Notes*, these had evolved into Flight Reference
Cards which governed the actions of the entire
crew and not just the pilots' procedures. The
Vulcan was much more advanced than its
predecessors, and it required a variety of quite
complex systems. Each of the nine flying control
surfaces were driven by an electrically powered
hydraulic motor, instead of the more usual
hydraulically powered systems. In addition,
instead of separate ailerons and elevators
customary in most aircraft, in the Vulcan B2
the pilot could operate all eight surfaces on the
trailing edges of the wings in both pitch and
roll to get maximum control at high altitude,
these surfaces were therefore called elevons.
There was no system of manual reversion for
operating the flying control surfaces; if a control
surface failed it would remain stationary and the
remaining surfaces were more than adequate to
operate the aircraft. As back-up for the electrical
system powered by four large engine-driven
alternators, it had an AAPP and a wind-driven
RAT to supply emergency power to ensure that
the aircraft could continue to be controlled even
after a catastrophic electrical failure.

On entering the Vulcan, one climbed the
ladder fixed to the emergency exit door and
entered a dark chamber with two skylights in
the roof. This was the rear crew's operating
compartment with three rearward facing seats
for, from port to starboard, the Air Electronics
Officer, the Navigator Plotter and the Navigator
Radar. Set into the bottom of the compartment
was the bomb aimer's window. There were no
ejection seats for the rear crew members. In
an emergency the entrance door became the
emergency escape chute.

To reach the pilots' seats it was necessary to
climb another short vertical ladder and squeeze
sideways into one of the two ejection seats. At
first sight the flight deck seemed very small, and
the most noticeable feature was the poor view
through the front three windscreen panels. The
view of the instrument panel was very good,
however, for instead of a control wheel that was
standard for a large aircraft at that time, each

pilot had a fighter-type stick fitted with an elevon trimmer, a radio transmit button, a feel relief button, an autopilot cut-out switch and a nose wheel steering button. The engine instruments were central to both pilots. They could be seen clearly, as could the fuel gauges below them.

Pilots immediately felt at home in the Vulcan cockpit, because everything required to fly the aircraft could be seen easily and reached from the captain's left-hand seat. The combination of the control stick, with the four centrally located engine throttle levers, made it a real delight to control.

At the top of the instrument panel was the control surface indicator. This represented the tail view of the aircraft, showing the positions of the eight elevons and the single rudder surface. These surfaces were switched on from a control panel on the captain's side, which contained the starter buttons and also the failure warning lights for each control surface motor. The positions of the control surfaces were checked on the ground by moving the stick and watching the control surface indicator. In flight, any problem with the flying controls could easily be spotted on this indicator.

Before any flight, the fuel load had to be determined. This total was displayed on the four fuel gauges split equally between the engines. There was a novel fuel control panel which could be pulled out from underneath the fuel gauges. This had all the switches for controlling the feeding of fuel from the aircraft's fourteen fuel tanks. The fuel flowing from the tanks was controlled automatically through two proportioners, which ensured that the plane's centre of gravity remained constant. There was a fuel centre of gravity indicator, to warn of any discrepancy.

ABOVE Red Flag exercise at Nellis AFB, Nevada. B2, XM652, is seen here with her crew access door open. In the background is XL426 wearing the markings of 617 Squadron. She was retained by the RAF in 1984 for air display purposes. *Jonathan Falconer collection*

Cockpit of Vulcan XL426. *Phil Whalley*

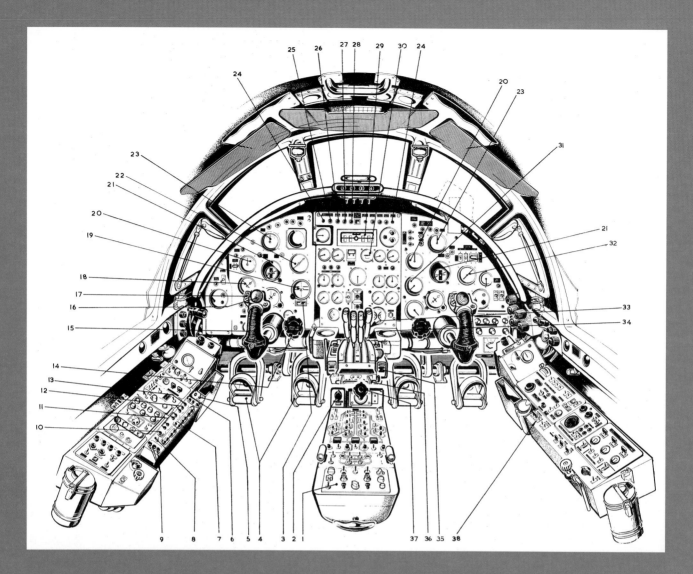

Vulcan cockpit

1   Auto-pilot control panel
2   Auto-pilot control
3   Side-slip indicator
4   Rudder pedals
5   Feel relief system isolation lock-in switch and indicator
6   Artificial feel failure indicator/push switches
7   PFC motor failure indicator/push switches
8   Yaw damper two-position toggle switch
9   PFC start push switches
10 Comparator reset
11 Pitch damper failure indicator/push switches

12 Auto-mach-trim, individual channel indicators
13 Auto-mach-trim, indicator push/pull switch
14 Adjuster, rudder pedals
15 Control handle, elevons
16 Elevon trim, four-way double-pole switch
17 Artificial feel relief cut-out switch
18 Altimeter Mk 19
19 Artificial Horizon (stand-by)
20 Air Speed Indicator
21 Director Horizon (Beam and GP)
22 Rate of Climb Indicator
23 Mach meter

24 Main warning system indicators
25 PFC unit failure
26 Artificial feel failure
27 Auto-stabilisers system failure
28 Air brakes
29 Control surface Indicator
30 Auto-pilot trim indicator
31 100,000ft altimeter
32 Climb and descent indicator
33 Rudder feel relief push switch
34 Rudder feel trim switch
35 Air brakes emergency switch
36 Air brakes selector switch
37 Emergency trim control
38 Auto-pilot reset switch

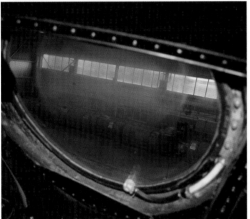

ABOVE Pilot and co-pilot at the controls of XH558 in flight. *Vulcan to the Sky Trust*

LEFT The circular portside crew window in the canopy. *Jonathan Falconer*

BELOW Left hand instrument panel. *Phil Whalley*

ABOVE Control column showing feel relief switch, elevon trimmer, press-to-transmit and nose-wheel steering buttons. *Phil Whalley*

BELOW Left side panel. *Phil Whalley*

ABOVE LEFT Autopilot bank control. *Phil Whalley*

ABOVE VHF radio set. *Jonathan Falconer*

LEFT Co-pilot at the controls of XH558. *Vulcan to the Sky Trust*

BELOW Right side panel. *Phil Whalley*

OPPOSITE TOP LEFT Fuel gauges. *Tony Blackman*

OPPOSITE TOP RIGHT Fuel panel. *Tony Blackman*

OPPOSITE Left-hand and centre instrument panels. *Phil Whalley*

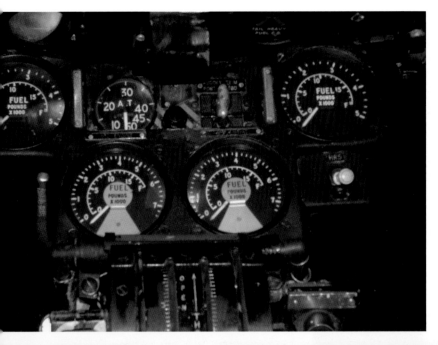

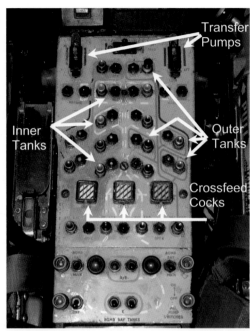

Transfer
Pumps

Inner
Tanks

Outer
Tanks

Crossfeed
Cocks

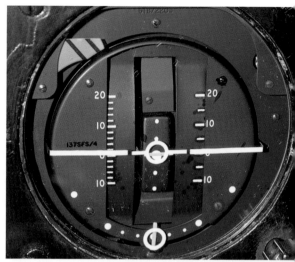

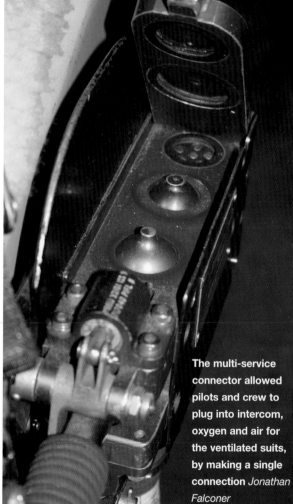

TOP LEFT First pilot's rudder bar and pedals. *Jonathan Falconer*

TOP RIGHT Director horizon. *Phil Whalley*

ABOVE CSDU oil temperature gauges. *Phil Whalley*

RIGHT Beam compass. *Phil Whalley*

The multi-service connector allowed pilots and crew to plug into intercom, oxygen and air for the ventilated suits, by making a single connection *Jonathan Falconer*

Learning to fly the Vulcan

Learning to fly the Vulcan was (and still is) a fascinating experience. Formal drills for key events, contained in the Flight Reference Cards, were vital to avoid errors and omissions and crew co-operation was particularly important.

On the early Vulcan B2s the Olympus engines were started, one at a time, using high pressure air from a trailer-mounted Paluste gas turbine, or from the AAPP fitted in the bomber's starboard wing root. Later aircraft had the additional option of a rapid starting system, using high pressure air from bottles in each engine bay. This system enabled all four engines to be started simultaneously, and the aircraft could commence taxiing within less than a minute. If required, four Vulcans on alert standby could be airborne within four minute of the order to scramble.

Taxiing the aircraft was straightforward, using the hydraulic nose wheel steering controlled by the button on the stick. Take-off was always a thrill, with the high power from the engines producing a large acceleration even at high weight and high temperatures. The stick was pulled back at the rotation speed, typically 145kts, raising the nose wheel. At unstick speed, 153kts, the aircraft leapt into the air accelerating rapidly. It was then necessary to enter the climb immediately, and initiate the retraction of the landing gear, before the aircraft reached its maximum undercarriage-down speed of 270kts.

The Vulcan was beautifully responsive during the climb, due to the effectiveness of the controls and the artificial feel systems. The latter prevented the pilot from over-controlling and perhaps over-stressing the aircraft. Lateral artificial feel was provided by a spring and also by mechanical stops, whose position varied with speed and so restricted the movement of the stick laterally. Fore and aft movement of the stick varied with the square of the speed, and simulated natural forces to a maximum of 150lb. The rudder artificial feel forces varied with cube of the speed. There was provision to turn off any artificial feel system, in the event of malfunction.

The initial cruise altitude of about 48,000ft and speed of .85 Mach was easy to maintain, as was the cruise climb of about 30ft/min. One unusual handling characteristic of the Vulcan was that it became unstable longitudinally as speed was increased above .86 Mach. To overcome that problem, Avro introduced a Mach trimmer that worked in series with the elevator circuit. When the trimmer was switched in, the aircraft felt stable as speed was increased, because the Mach trimmer applied more up-elevon than was actually needed. Consequently, as the speed increased further, it was necessary to push forward on the stick to keep the aircraft accelerating. At about .94 Mach the increase in the push force required became very marked. If the aircraft exceeded .95 Mach, the Mach trimmer was fully extended and the elevons were nearly fully up. If speed was increased beyond that point, it required a very large two-handed pulling force on the stick to prevent the aircraft entering a dive. For that reason, the maximum permitted speed for the Vulcan B2 was .92 Mach.

If the Mach trimmer was switched off, the pull force required became progressively greater at speeds above .86 Mach. Above .90 Mach it became heavier still, and very heavy indeed at .95 Mach with the stick almost fully back. For that reason the maximum permitted speed without a working Mach trimmer was .90 Mach.

Another unusual characteristic of the Vulcan was that at about .93 Mach the aircraft would execute an uncontrollable short period pitching oscillation, which increased rapidly and was uncontrollable. If it was not stopped immediately, it would cause the aircraft to break up. Consequently the aircraft was fitted with four pitch dampers, to ensure that this dangerous oscillation could not occur in squadron service. Only three pitch dampers were required to prevent the oscillation

occurring, however, so the failure of one pitch damper did not reduce the aircraft's maximum permitted speed. However, if a second pitch damper failed, speed had to be restricted to Mach .90.

ABOVE Gear up.

BELOW Blue Steel take-off. *Damien Burke*

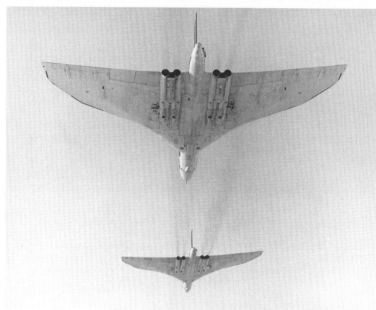

The aircraft was also fitted with two yaw dampers, to provide precise directional control. If both yaw dampers failed there was no speed restriction, but the aircraft was difficult to fly accurately and more rudder was required during manoeuvres.

At its maximum weight of 204,000lb, the Vulcan could start a cruise climb at 45,000ft. With an empty bomb bay and a light fuel load, it could reach 60,000ft. Its manoeuvrability at high altitude was second to none. Many a pilot of a high performance fighter was left looking through an empty windscreen at a clear blue sky, where once there had been a Vulcan.

Although the Vulcan had four engines it sometimes had to be considered as a twin engined aircraft, because the two engines on each side shared a common intake. This meant that if an engine surged at altitude, the adjacent engine would almost certainly fail also due to the disturbance of the intake flow into the other engine. Unless the engines could be relit immediately, it was necessary to drop below 30,000ft to get a relight.

Engine failures could occur for a variety of reasons but if, for example, there was a compressor blade failure, the blades would fly forward initially before being sucked into the other engine. So both engines would fail. Normally there was no problem flying the aircraft on two engines, though more rudder was required to counteract the asymmetric thrust.

TOP Vulcan at altitude.
IWM RAF T5723

ABOVE Vulcan
B2s of 50 and 101
Squadrons, based at
RAF Waddington, join
up during a training
exercise during 1975.
*Jonathan Falconer
collection*

RIGHT XH558 at
altitude, photographed
from the cockpit of a
Lightning T5. *Ian Black*

Military Flight System (MFS)

A special feature of the Vulcan was the Military Flight System (MFS), the first such system fitted into an RAF aircraft. This comprised a beam compass and a director horizon, both located in the pilots' instrument panel. For normal flying, the desired heading was set either manually on the beam compass or using information fed directly from the navigators' computer system. The director horizon served as a normal attitude indicator, but it had extra pointers to enable the pilot to follow the desired track and vertical paths. When the planned altitude was reached, the height lock would be engaged if the flight was to be made at a constant altitude. To maintain the desired flight path the pilot had merely to follow the pitch and attitude pointers on the MFS instruments, thereby removing the need for continually cross-referencing the heading on the compass and the height on the altimeter.

Terrain Following Radar –
Martin Withers, 'Black Buck' Vulcan pilot

Although the Vulcan was designed primarily as a high altitude bomber, it was also able to deliver attacks from low level carrying free-fall bombs or the Blue Steel stand-off missile. In this the pilot was assisted by the Terrain Following Radar (TFR), whose output fed directly into the MFS.

The procedure for flying at low level using TFR was straightforward. On the pilot's instrument panel was a height selector switch, on which he could set the datum flight altitude of the aircraft down to a minimum of 200ft. The TFR pod mounted in the extreme nose of the Vulcan continually measured the slant range to the nearest ground ahead of the aircraft, and compared this against the datum altitude selected. If the TFR sensed that the aircraft needed to climb or descend in order to maintain the datum altitude, it displayed this as a pitch demand on the MFS instrument.

Meanwhile, in the rear, the two navigators monitored the aircraft's track and compared this against the known hazards ahead. When azimuth corrections were required, these were fed into the beam compass of the MFS. Thus

ABOVE Vulcan B1A.

to follow the correct flight path at low altitude, the pilot flying the aircraft had simply to obey the pitch and azimuth commands displayed on the MFS.

TFR was easy to use, though it was important to appreciate the limitations of the system. Because of its inbuilt safety circuits, the radar could maintain the datum altitude only over mildly undulating terrain. The forward-looking narrow beam radar was incapable of detecting pylons or electrical wires or similar obstacles ahead of the aircraft. If the aircraft had a drift angle of more than 5 degrees, again it might fail to detect obstacles lying in its path. Moreover, at bank angles in excess of 20 degrees, the radar's performance was seriously degraded.

Yet, even with those limitations, the TFR gave the Vulcan a useful addition in capability. With its aid the aircraft could deliver attacks at low level at night or through cloud at speeds up to 350kts, making it a difficult target for enemy guns or missile systems.

BELOW XM606 over **Fylingdales.** *Jonathan Falconer collection*

ABOVE **Long finals.**
JCB

In the descent and landing

At the end of a flight at high altitude the aircraft would descend with the throttles closed and the air brakes extended, for the maximum rate of descent. The buffet from the air brakes was noticeable, but it was not uncomfortable even at maximum speed.

One thing that was noticeable when flying at low speed was that the elevons became less effective in roll. To stop adverse yaw being generated when applying roll control it was necessary to apply rudder at the same time to harmonise with the lateral control movement and thus minimise sideslip. Also, the nose started to rise significantly at the lower speeds, further reducing the downwards view. Thus the view on the landing approach was somewhat more restricted than on a conventional aircraft. Pilots soon got used to the poor view, however, and found the side window useful for checking their height off the ground just prior to touchdown.

At a typical landing weight, 140,000lb, the runway threshold speed was 135kts. Landing the Vulcan was always an interesting event. There were no flaps but the air brakes were

BELOW **Approach.**
Damien Burke

RIGHT Air brakes deployed. *Damien Burke*

CENTRE That was close! *Ian Waudby*

BOTTOM Touchdown. *JCB*

extended to give as much drag as possible. The power and rpm from the Olympus engines were sufficiently high to give a good response from the throttles, when more power was required. As the aircraft slowed down its nose rose, gradually obscuring the ground nearest to the aircraft.

The optimum way to land the Vulcan was to start the flare early, and keep pulling the stick back to prevent the wheels touching prematurely. The aircraft would then touchdown smoothly on its rear wheels, with the stick nearly fully back. The attitude of the aircraft was well nose up, so there was a lot of drag. The nose wheel could then be lowered on to the runway. Alternatively the stick could be kept fully back, in which case the nose would eventually drop gently on the tarmac as the speed reduced.

Normally very little braking was required to bring the aircraft to a halt, particularly if the nose was kept up for as long as possible. Although the aircraft carried a large brake parachute, this was rarely needed unless there was an emergency.

The flight-testing of XH558 – Tony Blackman

On the 23 June 1960 I carried out the final production flight-test schedule on Vulcan B2, XH558, destined to be the first Vulcan B2 for the RAF and the last Vulcan to fly. As was usual, the aircraft was not fitted with any weapons systems or radar. Our task at Avro was to check that the basic systems that operated the aircraft and made it safe to fly, were all working correctly. The actual schedule on XH558 does not remain in my memory. But, since I flew it only once, it must have been a normal production schedule without any special problems. However, because it was the first B2 production schedule, we would have made sure that nothing was forgotten in the written schedule we were using for the first time.

The Vulcan flight test crew was composed of four men: a test pilot, a flight-test observer or another pilot in the right-hand seat, an AEO to manage the electrical system and the navigation using a hyperbolic Gee Mk 3 receiver, and lastly the flight test observer who made sure that the schedule was completed, making notes as required.

The first thing we did after we were all strapped in was to check our intercom and the radios. The AEO started the Rover AAPP and checked the electric generation from its alternator. The system warning lights were checked in the front and back of the aircraft and the engines were then prepared for starting. At this stage of the production cycle XH558 had only the Olympus Mk 201 engines of 17,000lb thrust. These were not fitted with rapid engine start modification, so the engines had to be started one at a time. Our normal procedure was to start the first engine from the Paluste ground rig, the next engine from the AAPP and the other two engines by cross bleeding the air from the running engines by setting their power at 70 per cent rpm. On later aircraft, when the rapid start facility had been fitted, all four engines would be started at once from the air bottles.

The correct functioning of the automatic fuel feeding system from the fourteen tanks was very important, and at the same time the group and single tank fuel contents indication system needed checking. The contents of each tank were therefore recorded and also the position of the fuel centre of gravity on the cg indicator. While we recorded the fuel gauges, the AEO checked the functioning of the four engine-driven alternators to ensure the synchronisation system worked correctly.

Next the flying controls were started. The pilots checked the correct movement of the elevons and saw that the control surface indicator gave the correct indications, while the ground crew confirmed the movement of the control surfaces. The chocks were then removed and the aircraft taxied out. The nose wheel steering buttons on each control column were operated and the aircraft turned on to the runway. With the aircraft stationary and the foot brakes firmly applied, the throttles were advanced to 80 per cent. As the brakes were released, full power was applied while checking that the jet pipe temperatures and engine rpm were within limits.

We carried only about 40,000lb of fuel and nothing in the bomb bay, so the acceleration was very rapid. The aircraft had to be rotated to a fairly steep attitude, to ensure that the landing gear would be fully retracted before reaching its limiting speed of 270kts.

The pressurisation switch was turned on. Cruise power was selected on the engine take-off/cruise switch and the aircraft climbed to 55,000ft while monitoring the cabin pressure differential, the engine rpms and JPT (jet pipe temperature) readings on the climb.

During the climb the flying control feel and performance would be examined, plus correct functioning of the trimmer switches on the pilots' controls. That included lifting the trim button on the sticks, to ensure that both elevator switches and both aileron switches were needed to adjust the trim feel. The aircraft was levelled at 55,000ft and then cruised at Mach .85. Cross checks were made between the two pilots' instrument panels, to ensure there were no discrepancies. The autopilot was switched on and the height lock engaged to check satisfactory performance.

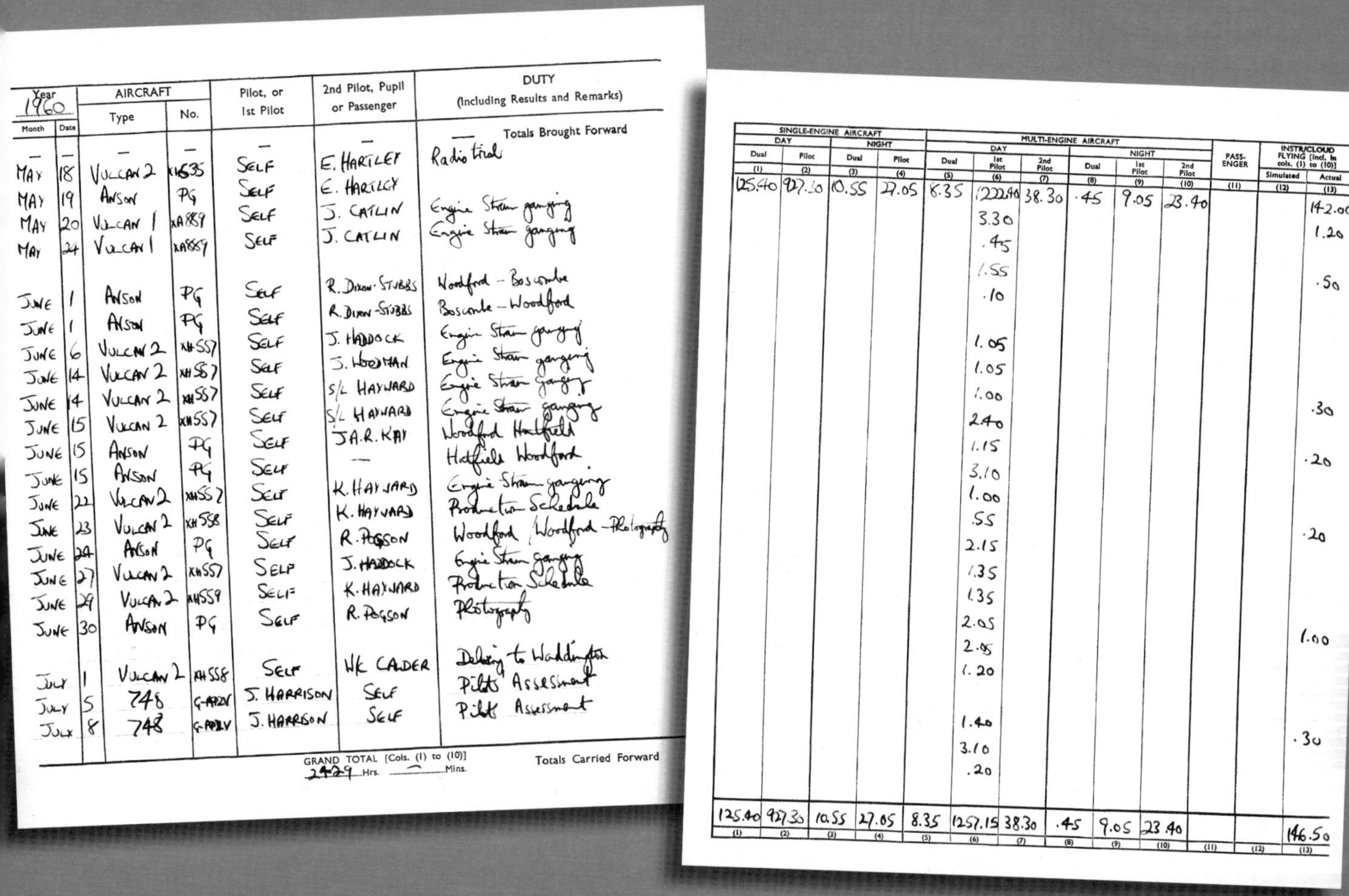

Left logbook page:

Year 1960 Month	Date	Aircraft Type	No.	Pilot, or 1st Pilot	2nd Pilot, Pupil or Passenger	DUTY (Including Results and Remarks)
						Totals Brought Forward
MAY	18	VULCAN 2	XH535	SELF	E. HARTLEY	Radio trial
MAY	19	ANSON	PG	SELF	E. HARTLEY	
MAY	20	VULCAN 1	XA889	SELF	J. CATLIN	Engine Strain gauging
MAY	24	VULCAN 1	XA889	SELF	J. CATLIN	Engine Strain gauging
JUNE	1	ANSON	PG	SELF	R. DIXON-STUBBS	Woodford – Boscombe
JUNE	1	ANSON	PG	SELF	R. DIXON-STUBBS	Boscombe – Woodford
JUNE	6	VULCAN 2	XH557	SELF	J. HADDOCK	Engine Strain gauging
JUNE	14	VULCAN 2	XH557	SELF	J. HOSTMAN	Engine Strain gauging
JUNE	14	VULCAN 2	XH557	SELF	S/L HAYWARD	Engine Strain gauging
JUNE	15	VULCAN 2	XH557	SELF	S/L HAYWARD	Engine Strain gauging
JUNE	15	ANSON	PG	SELF	J.A.R. KAY	Woodford Hatfield
JUNE	15	ANSON	PG	SELF	—	Hatfield Woodford
JUNE	22	VULCAN 2	XH557	SELF	K. HAYWARD	Engine Strain gauging
JUNE	23	VULCAN 2	XH558	SELF	K. HAYWARD	Production Schedule
JUNE	24	ANSON	PG	SELF	R. POGSON	Woodford, Woodford – Photography
JUNE	27	VULCAN 2	XH557	SELF	J. HADDOCK	Engine Strain gauging
JUNE	29	VULCAN 2	XH559	SELF	K. HAYWARD	Production Schedule
JUNE	30	ANSON	PG	SELF	R. POGSON	Photography
JULY	1	VULCAN 2	XH558	SELF	WK CALDER	Delivery to Waddington
JULY	5	748	G-ARAY	J. HARRISON	SELF	Pilots Assessment
JULY	8	748	G-ARMV	J. HARRISON	SELF	Pilots Assessment

GRAND TOTAL [Cols. (1) to (10)] 2429 Hrs. ——— Mins. Totals Carried Forward

Right logbook page:

	SINGLE-ENGINE AIRCRAFT				MULTI-ENGINE AIRCRAFT						PASS- ENGER	INSTR/CLOUD FLYING [Incl. in cols. (1) to (10)]	
	DAY		NIGHT		DAY			NIGHT					
	Dual	Pilot	Dual	Pilot	Dual	1st Pilot	2nd Pilot	Dual	1st Pilot	2nd Pilot		Simulated	Actual
	(1)	(2)	(3)	(4)	(5)	(6)	(7)	(8)	(9)	(10)	(11)	(12)	(13)
	125.40	927.30	10.55	27.05	8.35	1222.40	38.30	.45	9.05	23.40			142.00
						3.30							1.20
						.45							
						1.55							.50
						.10							
						1.05							
						1.05							
						1.00							.30
						2.40							
						1.15							.20
						3.10							
						1.00							
						.55							.20
						2.15							
						1.35							
						1.35							
						2.05							1.00
						2.45							
						1.20							
						1.40							
						3.10							.30
						.20							
	125.40	927.30	10.55	27.05	8.35	1257.15	38.30	.45	9.05	23.40			146.50
	(1)	(2)	(3)	(5)	(6)	(7)	(8)	(9)	(10)	(11)	(12)	(13)	

Slam accelerations were then carried out on each engine in turn, to make certain the engines did not surge and flame out.

The aircraft was accelerated to check the correct functioning of the Mach trimmer. At about Mach .88 a push force would be felt to keep the aircraft accelerating. By Mach .93 this push force would be very large. The aircraft was kept at this speed in a dive and two of the four pitch dampers were switched off, one at a time, to ensure that the dampers were working correctly. The high speed run was then repeated with the Mach trimmer turned off, to make sure the pull forces at the top Mach number were not excessively high. Next the aircraft was slowed to Mach .85 and the yaw damper checked.

The AEO would re-check the electrics and then the ram air turbine (RAT) was extended to check its correct functioning. The descent was continued to 30,000ft, when the AAPP was restarted and its alternator was used to take over the supplies from the RAT. Each engine was stopped in turn and re-lit. After that the aircraft descended to 15,000ft and the speed reduced until buffet was encountered. Again the pilots' instruments were cross checked at these low speeds. At 200kts the entrance door was opened to check correct functioning, and then closed again.

Fuel was transferred from No 7 to No 1 tanks and back to check the transfer pumps and the centre-of-gravity indicator. The radio altimeter was checked during the landing approach and touch-down. A roller landing was carried out, followed by a full stop landing streaming the tail brake parachute. Finally, before shutting down, a fuel check was carried out.

As this was the first Vulcan B2 for the RAF, I delivered it directly to No 230 Operational Conversion Unit at RAF Waddington on 1 July 1960.

Chapter 5

Navigator's View

'Jeff' Jefford

━━◉━━━━━━━━━━━━━━━━━━━━━

'Jeff' Jefford is the son of a long-serving RAF officer. He entered the RAF in 1959 and began training as a pilot, but quickly realised his mistake and re-mustered to navigator. On completion of his training he flew with 45 Squadron on Canberras, and then went on to 83 and 50 Squadrons with Vulcans. Jeff also served as a navigation instructor and amassed more than 3,500 flying hours by the time he retired from the Service with the rank of wing commander in 1991. He currently serves on the Executive Committee of the RAF Historical Society. Jeff is editor of the society's journal, and author of a number of books on the history of the RAF.

OPPOSITE Nav Plotter Sqn Ldr Maurice Patterson at work inside a Vulcan B2 of No 44 Squadron in 1979. Careful scrutiny of this photograph shows that the latitude and longitude displayed on the Ground Position Indicator corresponds with the map in front of the nav plotter – over Labrador and according to the Decca at 450kts ground speed. *Andy Leitch*

ABOVE Navigator at work in XH558. *Vulcan to the Sky Trust*

BELOW A general view of the two nav stations. While there was no 'trade demarcation' as such, it is generally true to say that the area on the left of the photo was the Nav Rad's playground, while that on the right was the Nav Plotter's affair, with a bit on the top of mutual interest. The toys on the right were the province of the AEO. *Glen Ambler*

tarting with the Canberra, one of the fundamentals of post-war Air Ministry bomber procurement policy appears to have been that, whenever possible, navigators were to be buried in the bowels of the aeroplane and denied any external visual reference. This policy prevailed for many years, and it seemed that the powers that be were persuaded to treat glass as a strategic commodity in short supply.

This was in marked contrast to the opposition's practice, the navigator's station on a typical Soviet bomber of the 1950s, the Ilyushin 28 and the Tupolev 16 for example. These had generously-glazed bay windows, providing a magnificent panoramic view of the passing countryside.

The ultimate expression of the British philosophy was manifested in the V-bombers whose navigators were required not only to work in the dark, but to do it facing backwards. That led to spatial disorientation and provided bags of scope for misunderstandings as to whether a left turn meant 'My left, or yours?'.

The rules of the game were simple – navigators were supposed to estimate where

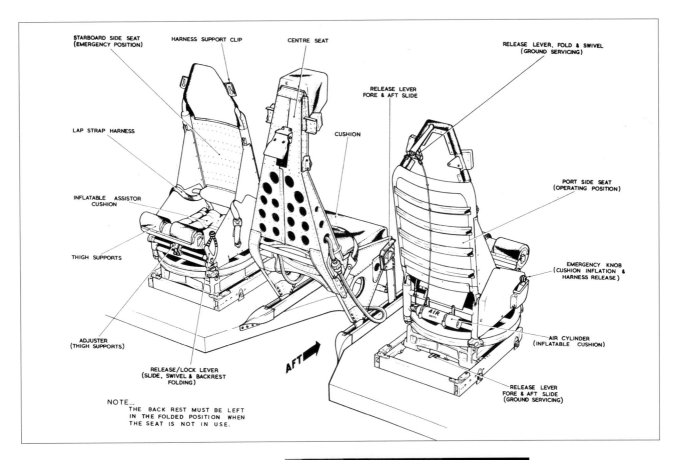

STARBOARD SIDE SEAT
(EMERGENCY POSITION)

HARNESS SUPPORT CLIP

CENTRE SEAT

RELEASE LEVER, FOLD & SWIVEL
(GROUND SERVICING)

RELEASE LEVER
FORE & AFT SLIDE

LAP STRAP HARNESS

CUSHION

PORT SIDE SEAT
(OPERATING POSITION)

INFLATABLE ASSISTOR
CUSHION

THIGH SUPPORTS

EMERGENCY KNOB
(CUSHION INFLATION &
HARNESS RELEASE)

ADJUSTER
(THIGH SUPPORTS)

AIR CYLINDER
(INFLATABLE CUSHION)

RELEASE/LOCK LEVER
(SLIDE, SWIVEL & BACKREST
FOLDING)

AFT

RELEASE LEVER
FORE & AFT SLIDE
(GROUND SERVICING)

NOTE...
THE BACK REST MUST BE LEFT
IN THE FOLDED POSITION WHEN
THE SEAT IS NOT IN USE.

the aeroplane *might* be and every now and then, and would announce this to Biggles in the front. The latter would then look out of his window and award the guess with marks out of ten.

This may be a fanciful interpretation but it is a fact that for several years this particular navigator was fortunate enough to fly over much of the world, courtesy of the RAF's Canberras and Vulcans, without actually having been able to see very much of it.

During the quarter century that the Vulcan flew with the RAF, the art of practical air navigation was transformed into a science. When it entered service in the 1950s, the aircraft required two men to monitor and manage its state-of-the-art navigation and bombing equipment. They had also to handle any of the potential failures to which the kit was prone, while guiding the aeroplane to its destination and, if appropriate, dropping a bomb on it.

By the 1980s the Vulcan's equipment had been updated somewhat, but it was still an analogue system based on 1950's (even in

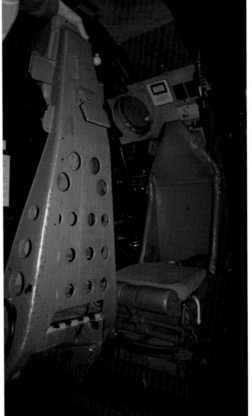

Jonathan Falconer

ABOVE AND LEFT
To assist in a rapid escape from the aircraft the Nav Rad and the AEO could rotate their seats to face forwards. All three crew seats also had cushions inflated using compressed air to assist the men to stand up if the aircraft was pulling 'G'.

ABOVE Nav radar station. The Nav Rad's area was dominated by the Indicator Type 301, the H2S cathode ray tube and its associated controls for adjusting the picture. The box above it was an R88 camera, which could photograph the screen. In front of the Indicator 301 was the Control Unit (CU) 626 – a 'joystick', which was used to 'move the picture around'. On a bombing run the CU626 was connected to the autopilot, so the Nav Rad could actually steer the aircraft to the bomb release point. The Indicator 301 was flanked by the CU595 to the left and the CU585 to the right. The CU595 permitted the 'tilt' of the aerial to be altered, and controlled the direction and arc of sector scan. The CU585 was used to select the functions offered by the NBC ('fix', 'stab', 'home' or 'bomb') and provided a means of inserting 'internal' offsets of up to 20,000yds north/south and east/west; a second set of 'external' offsets, of up to 40,000yds was available via the CU12558, which was fitted in the desk under a removable lid.

The circular unit mounted on the upper panel was the Radar Altimeter Mk 6A. Most of the dials to its left were temperature read-outs from the bomb bay, to do with Blue Steel. The dial at the top was a pressure read-out associated with the NBC.

The large 'shared' panel on the far right of the picture, the so-called 'Nav Panel', displayed the information being used/produced by the NBC, including track, ground speed or true air speed, and the wind velocity, expressed in its north/south and east/west components.

While most of the Nav Rad's kit stayed the same throughout the life of the Vulcan, the Nav Plotter's displays changed over time. Only two of these black boxes would still be present in a similar photograph taken ten years later. Taking the Plotter's panel from the bottom and working up, the first two boxes are, on the left, Green Satin Mk 2 (a Doppler navigation system) and the GPI (Ground Position Indicator) Mk 6. Above them are on the left, GEE Mk 3 (with the small circular screen and sundry knobs and tits below); in the centre the Inertial Navigation Control Unit; and on the right the Store Control Panel, both of the latter being concerned with the missile. There was a third missile box (the Inertial Navigation Monitoring Unit) located, somewhat inconveniently, under the lid of the Plotter's desk. On the canted, upper panel the individual dial displayed forward throw (for free-fall bombing), flanked by the Track Control Unit (which combined magnetic heading with variation and drift to provide an output of true track, which was used, among other things, to orientate the H2S display). Above were four dials displaying indicated air speed, altitude, true track and outside air temperature. The top row comprised a relative bearing indicator (ie, the read-out from the radio compass and four fuel contents gauges. *Phil Whalley*

places 1940's) technology. By the 1980s any self-respecting combat aeroplane had a remarkably accurate digital navigation/attack computer supported by an inertial platform and/or a solid state Doppler radar, the overall system having an insignificant failure rate. Pending the air force's finding the money for a fleet fit, the contemporary navigator was probably saving up his pocket money to buy a personal Global Positioning System from a shop in the local High Street.

So what did the passage of those twenty-five years mean for the average Vulcan navigator, or pair of navigators? The Navigator Radar is the easier of the two to discuss, because during this period his kit did not change significantly. He was responsible for operating the H2S Mk 9A radar, the result of a dozen years of development work applied to the H2S Mk 1 of the Second World War. It could provide fixes to a notional accuracy of the order of 200yds and could deliver bombs within about 400yds, although a high degree of skill was required in order to achieve consistently good results.

When attacking a target that did not show up on radar, it was possible to use another object, one that would give a positive radar return, nearby. By measuring the north/south and east/west distances (up to a maximum of 40,000yds in each plane) between the target and the selected response, and inserting these into the equipment, the Navigator Radar aimed at the 'offset' response, while the aeroplane actually tracked towards the real target.

The north-oriented radar picture was displayed on a nine-inch diameter cathode ray tube and could be 'stabilised', that is to say fed with groundspeed so that the ground appeared to stand still while the centre of scan, the 'aeroplane', moved across it. The rotation of the six-foot wide radar scanner could be restricted so that it scanned only a narrow sector, rather than the full 360°, thus minimising the radiation that could betray the aircraft's presence. It also increased the frequency with which a particular response was illuminated.

The display could be viewed at a variety of scales between 1:1 million and 1:1/8 million. At high level the radar could paint a map with a radius of about 180 miles. At the other extreme, the set could be adjusted so that an airfield

response (often the actual runway but, if not, at least the adjacent hangars) was about 2in long – certainly good enough to make a reasonable stab at an approach.

Allied to the H2S radar was the Navigation and Bombing Computer (NBC). This did exactly what its name suggests. And while the radar itself was relatively trouble-free, the computer elements, several dustbin-sized containers full of gears, cams, bicycle chains, pieces of 35mm film, electrical relays and so on, could cause problems. There were many ways these 'calculators', as they were known, could fail. For each such failure there was a specific limited procedure which required the Navigator Radar to compensate for the malfunction. Since bomb-aiming with a 100 per cent serviceable set of equipment was 'easy', the routine training programme dictated that a large proportion of practice attacks had to be carried out using these fall-back options.

At low level, apart from providing fixes, the H2S could also assist in terrain-following at night or in poor visibility, since any ground ahead of, and higher than, the aircraft would obscure returns from more distant features – a so-called 'cut-off' situation. When this occurred, the pilot was advised to climb until the aircraft was high enough to permit the radar to 'see' past the obstruction to the next feature, thus ensuring that it would fly over, rather than into, the first one.

While the Navigator Radar's equipment may not have changed very much over the years, the weapons did and he was the designated weapons expert within the crew. The Vulcan B1s carried a Blue Danube nuclear weapon, or the Violet Club, or American-supplied Mk 5 thermonuclear weapon.

ABOVE Nav radar Flt Lt Jerry Gegg at work in the rear compartment of a No 44 Squadron Vulcan B2. *Andy Leitch*

BELOW Navigator's joystick. *Phil Whalley*

By the time the Vulcan B 2 entered service, these early arrangements had been superseded by the home-grown Yellow Sun Mks 1 and 2, followed, on three squadrons, by the Blue Steel stand-off missile. All of these being progressively replaced by the WE177 weapon during the 1960s. Training flights, simulating all of the safety precautions and controlled release procedures associated with such weapons, were flown using dummy rounds.

Initially, bombing accuracy was assessed by ground-based radar units. Once the force had adopted wholesale the 'below the radar' low level tactics, bombing scores were based on vertical photographs taken by a camera installed at the visual bomb-aiming station.

For the conventional bombing role, the bomb bay could accommodate up to twenty-one 1,000lb 'iron' bombs which could be dropped singly or as a stick of variable length. There was a range of fuses and tail units to permit detonation above, on contact with or below the surface as required. Live bombing practice was carried out using 25lb (later 28lb) practice bombs, plus an occasional allocation of 1,000-pounders.

Visual aiming was done (by the other navigator) using a T4 bombsight, although this procedure was only practical at medium or high level. With the adoption, almost exclusively, of low-level tactics, visual aiming had largely given way to radar-aiming by the mid-1960s. Conventional bombing was gradually allowed to fade away, however. Few, if any, 1,000-pounders were provided in the 1970s, and the commitment was quietly dropped altogether in 1980 – two years before it was

actually needed, at very short notice, in the Falklands Conflict.

Unlike that available to the Navigator Radar, the equipment provided for the other navigator, the Navigator Plotter, did change over time. In the early days he was able to monitor the aircraft's progress via a Ground Position Indicator (GPI) Mk 4A furnished with heading from a magnetically monitored gyro-compass, using velocities from a Green Satin Doppler radar. The accuracy of the aircraft's computed position decayed with time, so the GPI was periodically reset against fixes obtained from H2S or GEE Mk 3. More traditional navigational aids included astro navigation and a Marconi AD7092D radio compass.

By the mid-1960s GEE had been supplanted by TACAN, the Doppler had been upgraded to the Green Satin Mk 2, and the original GPI was being replaced by the Mk 6. Designed and built by Elliott Bros, the GPI Mk 6 probably represented the pinnacle of analogue computing technology. Tailored to meet the specific demands of the Blue Steel stand-off missile system, it eventually became a standard fit for all Vulcans including free-fall aircraft.

Blue Steel represented a significant technological advance in that it introduced the RAF's first inertial platform. Also, until the missile was released, the platform's output was available to the navigator in the carrier aircraft and he could integrate this with information from other sources. Because the missile's free flight time would be measured only in minutes, long-term accuracy was not a requirement. So long as the missile was on board, therefore, the platform was effectively slaved to the output of the aircraft's Doppler equipment. However, whenever the Doppler 'unlocked' the platform became the primary source. Conversely, the heading output of the platform was far more accurate than that provided by the, essentially magnetic, compass system in the aircraft.

The need to upgrade the heading source had long been recognised and by the late 1960s, just as Blue Steel was being withdrawn, the gyro-magnetic compass was being progressively complemented by the Heading Reference System Mk 2, which was purely gyro-based and very accurate. This eventually became the standard fleet fit, thus providing all

Vulcans with the precise heading information that had previously been confined to the missile carriers. At much the same time the means of measuring drift and groundspeed had been further improved by the introduction of Decca Doppler 72. The new Doppler system was a solid-state device with no moving parts, which went some way towards eliminating the less desirable characteristics of the, occasionally temperamental, Green Satin it replaced.

So much for the equipment; what of the procedures? So long as all of the kit performed to specification, an operational sortie should have been no problem at all. With the GPI being fed by the Doppler, and with its read-out periodically refined by H2S fixes, a Vulcan crew could have found its way to any target within range. And it could be hit with a more than adequate degree of precision, bearing in mind that the aircraft was delivering a nuclear weapon.

The snag was that the kit was prone to failure, which meant that it would often be necessary to revert to limited procedures. As a result, in the course of routine training, both navigators tended to spend much of their time working with one hand tied behind their backs. Reference has already been made to the Navigator Radar having to cope with equipment failures, some of which could degrade navigational information. Also the Navigator Plotter's life could be further complicated by the loss of Doppler, problems with the Blue Steel's inertial system, and so on. There were specific procedures laid down to paper over virtually any combination of cracks. Most training sorties involved at least one element of dealing with a failure of some kind, often real, sometimes simulated.

While the TACAN would be routinely selected to a convenient station as a safety precaution, apart from international transits or airways flying, it was little used in practice because it was vulnerable to jamming and so was unlikely to be available on a war sortie.

At distances greater than about 200 miles from land, astro navigation became the primary fixing aid. Astro navigation had definite limitations, especially by day when, as often as not, the only available celestial body was the Sun. And it could furnish only a single position

line. By night, calculating, shooting and plotting a classic two-star, seven-shot fix required *at least* twenty minutes from start to finish. It was a laborious process, involving numerous arithmetical processes, and any numerical error might negate the whole exercise. Much has been claimed with regard to the accuracy of astro navigation, but much of it has been exaggerated. That is not to say that remarkable results were never achieved; they were. But the overall performance of this method was far less spectacular than the best. For instance, while the final error of the winning crew in the annual Bomber Command Navigation Competition was usually measured in yards, the average accuracy was more conveniently measured in miles – and sometimes quite a lot of them. That said, so long as astro was available you were never 'lost'; but that is not the same as saying that you knew precisely where you were.

ABOVE XM652 of 44 Squadron at Nellis AFB during a Red Flag combat training exercise in the late 1970s. *Jonathan Falconer collection*

BELOW Vulcan B2, XM606, flies over Fylingdales early warning radar site in the Yorkshire Dales in 1973. XM606 was one of four Vulcans that competed against the US Air Force in exercise Giant Voice, a navigation and bombing competition held at Barksdale AFB, Louisiana. *Jonathan Falconer collection*

Chapter 6

The AEO's View

Alfred Price

In May 1962, having completed the Vulcan B2 conversion course at RAF Finningley, Alfred Price joined No 9 Squadron at RAF Coningsby as an Air Electronics Officer. At that time the squadron was re-equipping with Vulcan B2s, having previously flown Canberras. During the next seven years he logged 1,520 flying hours in Vulcans, including five flights totalling 18 hours in XH558. He retired from the RAF in 1974 to concentrate on his writing career and is now the published author of more than 50 aviation books.

OPPOSITE Vulcan B2, XM571, of the Scampton Wing, with the doors to the ECM bulge open so the Vapour Cycle Cooling Pack (VCCP) can be topped up with Freon refrigerant. On the starboard side of the ECM bulge is the exhaust for the cooling air, after it had passed through the radiator, to carry away the heat. *IWM RAF T4845*

RIGHT Co-author
Alfred Price, as a
young flight lieutenant
AEO in 1963. *Alfred
Price*

When I joined the V-Force it was committed to the high altitude penetration and weapon delivery mode. Our training in the Vulcan B2 was focused on delivering a Yellow Sun Mk 2 megaton range free-fall thermonuclear weapon on a target, released from altitudes around 56,000ft. Our aircraft were brand new machines which we collected from the makers. Like the other V-bombers they were painted in brilliant anti-flash white overall. So, almost inevitably, the 'Deterrent Force' became known as the 'Detergent Force'.

In the previous chapter, 'Jeff' Jefford alluded to the unnatural working environment for the rear crew members in the Vulcan: flying backwards, unable to see out and in a darkened cabin. Different people reacted to these factors in different ways. For my part I was not particularly put out either by flying backwards or being unable to see out. But I did find the deliberately darkened cabin a bit disconcerting for a while.

Stalwart member of the navigators' union that he is, 'Jeff' loyally omitted to mention that the demand for the darkened rear cabin came entirely from the Navigator Radars' empire. They needed that degree of darkness to get the optimum possible contrast on the radar picture, so they could pick out their radar offset points.

On a combat mission the AEO's main task

BELOW The AEO's position of a combat ready Vulcan aircraft in the early 1960s. Along the right side of the image, mounted on the cabin wall, are the controls for the electrical alternators and other power supplies. At the bottom, mounted on the AEO's table, is the Morse key. Then, from right to left abutting the table, are the intercom control box, the combined control unit for the three Red Shrimp noise jammers, the control unit for the Blue Saga radar warning receiver and that for the STR18 high frequency radio. The control unit above the STR18 is part of the Navigator/Plotter's territory. Above the Blue Saga control unit is the combined control unit for the two Blue Diver noise jammers, above that the Red Steer tail warning radar, and above that the control units for the Chaff and Rope dispensers. Above the Red Shrimp control unit is that for the Green Palm communications jammer, and above that the IFF (Identification Friend or Foe) system and its associated coding unit. *Alfred Price collection*

BELOW View of the rear crew compartment in XH558, looking towards the AEO's position. *Vulcan to the Sky Trust*

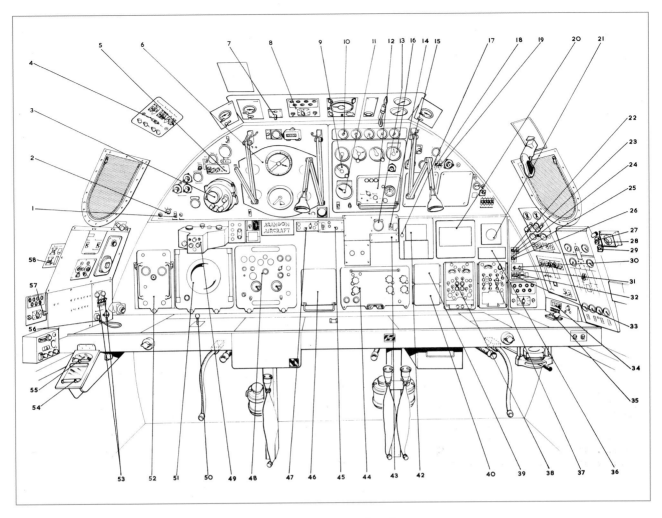

ABOVE Radar, radio and associated equipment in the rear crew compartment.

1. Scanner rotation control
2. Scanner stabilisation switch
3. Pulse altimeter
4. Radio control panel
5. True airspeed control panel
6. Navigation panel
7. Variable airspeed unit
8. Intercom control unit (nav/radar op)
9. Compass repeater – true magnetic heading
10. DF bearing indicator
11. Radio altimeter
12. Track controller unit, MFS
13. Indicator, Type 9547
14. Change-over switch
15. Dimmer switch – auto-land and TCU lights
16. Pilots' direction indicator
17. Fail indicator
18. Compass isolation switch – port

19. Compass isolation switch – starboard
20. Indicator, azimuth range
21. Indicator, Type 17171
22. Supplies switch
23. Output switch
24. Supply switch
25. Press-to-transmit switch
26. Conference intercom master switch
27. On/off switch
28. Control unit, Type 705
29. Auto throttle – on/off switch
30. Dimmer switch control unit dial lighting
31. Dimmer switch control unit dial lighting
32. Intercom master control switch
33. External intercom switches
34. ECM power supply control panel
35. Morse key
36. Control unit, Type 17172
37. Control unit, Type 9422
38. Control unit, Type 13044

39. Control transmitter/receiver, Type M53
40. Antenna control unit
41. Deleted (MOD 2501)
42. Control unit, Type 16929
43. Control unit, Type 7750
44. GPI Mk 6
45. HRU power failure indicator
46. Indicator control unit, Type 9869
47. Ground speed selector unit
48. Control unit, Type 585
49. Camera, Type RX88
50. Control unit, Type 626
51. Indicating unit, Type 301
52. Control unit, Type 595
53. NBC isolation indicators
54. Control unit, Type 12580
55. Bombing selector switch
56. NBC simulator socket
57. Intercom control unit – nav/air bomber
58. Simulated bombing panel

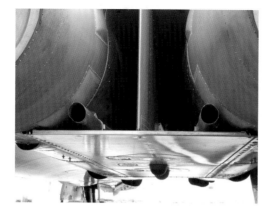

was to manage the electronic countermeasures (ECM) systems which constituted the bomber's sole means of self defence. Essentially the tactics with their systems can be summed up as; try either to conceal your real position, or else try to persuade the enemy you are somewhere else. Initially the Vulcan's electronic countermeasures (ECM) suite comprised:

- **Red Shrimp** high powered carcinotron noise jammer, three carried, operating in the DE band. The main units were located in the ECM bulge in the tail of the aircraft. These jammers were targeted at the Soviet Fansong (in each case the designations of Soviet equipment are given here by their NATO code names) missile guidance radar, which formed part of the SA-2 surface to air missile system. They also had a capability

against long range surveillance and Ground Controlled Intercept (GCI) radars operating in the DE band.

- **Blue Diver** high powered noise jammers, two carried, operating in the VHF band. Again, the main units were located in the ECM bulge in the tail of the aircraft. These were targeted at the Soviet Knife Rest and other VHF radars, which guided the Fansong missile guidance radars on to their targets.

- One **Green Palm** VHF noise jammer, main unit located in the ECM bulge in the tail, targeted at the Soviet fighter ground to air control channels. This jammer radiated an intentionally irritating note, a cross between badly played bagpipes and a police siren. Unfortunately, whenever the Green Palm was switched to transmit, that highly irritating note leaked into the Vulcan's intercom system where it hindered inter-crew communication. That breakthrough noise would was hardly suitable as mood music for the opening of the Third World War, and as Green Palm had other shortcomings it was soon removed from V-Bombers early on.

- **Blue Saga** radar warning receivers, with four sets of aerials mounted around the bomber to provide all-round cover. The system gave warning when an enemy DE band (surface-to-air missile) or an I-Band (fighter airborne intercept) radar scanned through the bomber or, more dangerously, locked on to it.

■ **Red Steer** tail warning radar mounted in the extreme tail, provided warning of enemy fighters entering the bomber's rear quadrant.

■ **Chaff, Rope** single packets of Chaff and Rope would be released at random intervals to provide a confusion factor for the enemy fighter control system, during the bombers' penetration and withdrawal. If a fighter was observed in the field of view of Red Steer, the AEO would instruct the pilot to turn sharply into the attacker, thereby exploiting the Vulcan's excellent turning ability at high altitude (the early Soviet air to air missiles were effective only when launched in the target's rear quadrant). While this was happening, the AEO had various tactics he could use to shake off the attacker. One that had proved effective was release a single bundle of I-Band Chaff followed about 5 second later by another. That would present the fighter pilot with a choice of targets: two easy ones (the Chaff clouds) or one difficult target (the manoeuvring bomber). Although the temptation was great, an over-enthusiastic release of Chaff at that time was not to be recommended. That would produce a dense trail, with the Vulcan at the front, which would fool nobody. The aim was to prevent the fighter from moving into a position behind the bomber where it could get off a missile shot. If the fighter

pilot succeeded in locking his radar on to the Vulcan, the time for finesse was over. Now the AEO would release Chaff at the maximum rate, while the pilot continued his maximum rate turn trying to keep the bomber outside the fighter's firing bracket. Such a confrontation at 56,000ft would not last long before the fighter, with its much higher wing loading, fell out of the sky.

BELOW 'Rope', dropped to confuse long wavelength ground radars. The packet, similar in size to the one above, contained three such reels of metal foil. When the packet was released the three reels fell away then unwound, each supported at one end by the small square 'parachute', to produce three vertical strips of foil suspended in the sky. Together, these three lengths of metal foil produced a radar echo similar to that from a Vulcan. *Alfred Price collection*

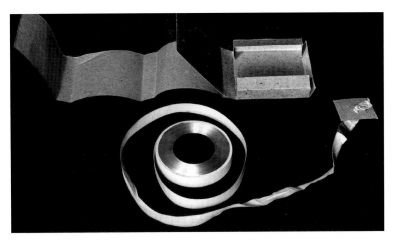

DE-Band Chaff would also be effective, in conjunction with noise jamming and a manoeuvre, against the SA-2 missile system. When flying through a missile defended area the bomber would engage in the 'Type 2A Manoeuvre', that is to say flying a zigzag

path. The AEO would jam with Red Shrimp during the straight legs, then cease jamming during each turn and release a few bundles of Chaff. On the next straight leg he would cease dropping Chaff, and resume jamming with Red Shrimp. These tactics had been tested against 'Blank Stare', a 'Fansong clone' built by the US Air Force, and had been found to be effective.

Strictly speaking, the Vapour Cycle Cooling Pack (VCCP) was not an item of ECM equipment, though it played a vitally important role in allowing the noise jammers to function properly. When a noise jammer transmitted, only about 8 per cent of the input power was radiated down the aerial. The remaining 92 per cent of the input power remained in the transmitter, and without an effective cooling system the transmitters would quickly overheat and burn out. The VCCP was a powerful cooling system located in the ECM bulge in the tail. This carried the excess heat away from the jammers, to the condenser on the starboard side of the ECM blister, and dissipated it in the airflow.

The early 1960s saw a proliferation of surface-to-air missile batteries in front of targets in the Soviet Union, and the introduction of

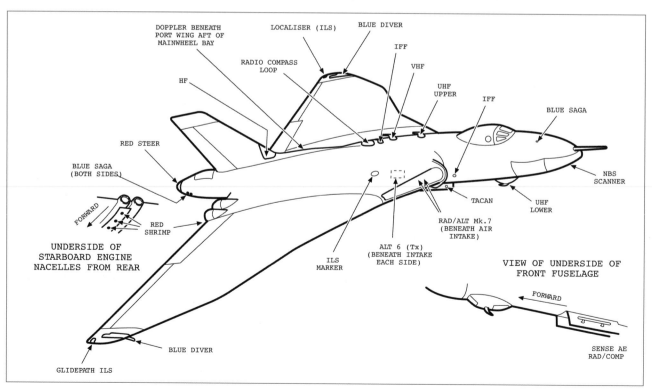

new systems. Simultaneously, the Soviet Air Force began a large scale deployment of Mach 2 fighters equipped with the modern air-to-air missiles, which could engage bombers at high altitude. Taken together, these factors meant that even with the available ECM systems, the V-bombers' ability to penetrate to targets at high altitude was slowly ebbing away. The defences against low altitude attackers were also being strengthened, though not at such a rate. On balance it seemed that the low altitude mode of attack, with bombers penetrating at altitudes below 1,000ft, would give bombers the greater probability of reaching their targets than the previous high level penetrations. The change over, from a Hi-Hi-Hi penetration to a Hi-Lo-Hi, was done in stages. First the Valiant force moved to the low altitude penetration, in 1961. Then the B1A Vulcans and Victors made the change, in March 1963. Finally, in the spring of 1964, the B2 Vulcans and Victors followed suit.

As air crews soon discovered, a whole different world faced them at low altitude. The AEO, in particular, found that few of the Vulcan's self-protection systems worked as effectively as before. The capability of the Red Shrimp and Blue Diver noise jammers was much reduced, since the undulations in the ground

that shielded the bombers from the defences, also shielded the enemy ground radars from the jamming. Similarly, dropping Chaff in the confusion role was a useless measure against ground radars that were themselves afflicted by ground returns.

ABOVE AEO Flt Lt Dick de Verteuil at work inside a Vulcan B2 of No 44 Squadron in 1979. *Andy Leitch*

LEFT A close-up view of the AEO's electrical control panels. On the right, the 200 volt 400 c/s generation controls; at the top left, the AAPP control panel; below it, the transformer rectifier panel which supplied direct current for some of the equipment. At the bottom are the power-on buttons for the various high-powered ECM systems. *Phil Whalley*

Worst affected was Red Steer tail warning radar. At high altitude this device had been reasonably effective. But low down, the returns from the ground swamped out the echoes from an approaching fighter. It was said, only half in jest, that at low altitude this radar was impossible to jam – because nothing an enemy could do would make the picture on the screen any worse than it already was!

This problem was not confined to one side, however, for the Soviet fighters' pulsed radars were also vulnerable to this effect. Sending fighters out to patrol lines to conduct visual searches for incoming bombers would have faced their own problems. The brilliant flashes from detonating nuclear warheads could cause temporary or even permanent damage to the eyesight of anyone looking at, or nearly at, an explosion from scores of miles away. The 'bottom line' was that during the mid 1960s the Soviet Air Defence system was quite unable to cope with a massed attack by low flying bombers.

To aid the V-bombers during their low

altitude penetrations, some new ECM systems were introduced. The Red Steer Mk 1 was replaced by the Red Steer Mk 2, fitted with a new scanning system that got rid of the worst of the ground returns. There was a new I-Band jammer, a new and much more effective radar warning receiver, and a dispensing system for infra red decoys.

It was a good try, but it was not good enough to restore the balance of effectiveness. By the late 1960s the Soviet Air Defence system had improved at an even faster rate. It had newer and more effective fighters, fighter radars and air-to-air and surface-to-air missile systems. Moreover, in June 1969, Britain's strategic nuclear passed to the Royal Navy, in the shape of its four submarines fitted with the Polaris ballistic missile system.

From then on the supply of money to improve the Vulcan's operational capability dried up almost completely.

* * *

Before we leave the AEO's viewpoint, there are two other duties for which he was responsible, those of managing the aircraft's communications and its electrical generation system.

Initially the Vulcan B 2 carried a communications suite comprising the following:
- an STR 18B HF radio
- two TR 1984/1986 VHF radios
- an ARC-52 UHF radio.
- a Marconi AD7092D radio compass (receive only)

The communications task was relatively simple, but that did not belie its extreme importance if the V-Force was ever launched in anger. Had the force been scrambled carrying nuclear weapons, the bombers would head eastwards on their pre-planned war routes. There still remained one option to halt the procedure, however. The bombers were not permitted to pass the 8 degrees east line of longitude, which runs just off the west coast of Denmark, unless they had received the correctly coded 'Go' signal. That signal would have been transmitted simultaneously on specified frequencies in the medium frequency (MF), high frequency (HF), very high frequency (VHF) and Ultra High Frequency (UHF) bands.

On most war targets the Vulcans would

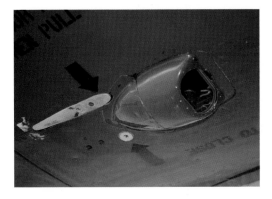

ABOVE AND LEFT **Located on the underside of the fuselage, just behind the main entrance door, is the lower head for the periscopic observation system. By means of a lever in the AEO's position, the latter is able to observe most of the underside of the aircraft. A similar periscopic window, mounted behind the cockpit canopy, allows the AEO to examine the upper side of the aircraft.** *Jonathan Falconer/ Phil Whalley*

have had little fuel in reserve, so there could be no question of hanging about at the 'Go' line waiting for something to happen. If the 'Go' signal was not received when the bombers reached the 'Go' line, they were to turn around and return to base.

As well as the flying controls and other systems, the Vulcan B2 electrical system generated the power to run the electronic countermeasures suite. Four large engine-driven alternators, each producing 200 volts at 400 cycles alternating current and rated at 40kVA, constituted the main part of the Vulcan B2 electrical system. In case of a major electrical failure, for example as a result of battle damage, the aircraft had two back-up electrical generation systems. The AAPP was a small jet engine which supplied emergency electrical power at altitudes up to 20,000ft. There was also a RAT – a wind driven propeller – which could be lowered into the airflow to provided emergency supply above that altitude.

In my experience the Vulcan B2 electrical system functioned perfectly reliably if it was left alone to run itself in the automatic mode. I never had any trouble with it, and if anyone did it was usually due to mishandling of the system.

The Vulcan, Stealth Bomber?

In recent years several publications – and even TV programmes on the Vulcan – have repeated the canard that the aircraft's aerodynamic shape in some way conferred upon it a measure of 'stealth', giving it a very low signature on radar. It has been said this factor enabled the Vulcan to penetrate an enemy air defence system without being detected. If only it could…

Assuredly that is not the case, however. Any coincidental resemblance between the Vulcan and the F-117 or the B-2 bomber –

which really are stealth aircraft – is just that, coincidental.

At the time the Vulcan was designed in the late 1940s, the concept of stealth was unknown. It would take decades of imaginative shaping, careful experimentation with exotic materials and construction to very fine tolerances, to bring a real 'low observables' aircraft into being.

In truth the Vulcan, like other large aircraft of its time, possessed a large radar signature. In its day it was a great aircraft, but we do not enhance its reputation by ascribing to it capabilities it never had.

BELOW **The AEO's position in the restored XH558, with the control units for the operational equipment removed. At the top left is retained the list of names of the team of RAF volunteers who looked after the aircraft during her final days in RAF service.** *Phil Whalley*

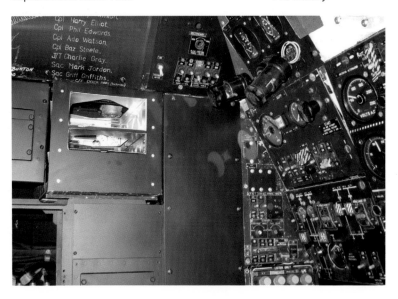

Chapter 7

The Crew Chief's View

Tony Regan

After leaving school Tony Regan
served a three-year apprenticeship
at what was then known as the
Bristol Aero Engine Company. He
then joined the RAF as an engine
fitter and worked on Canberras
and Victors. In 1968 he was posted
to RAF Waddington and from
then until 1971 he served as Crew
Chief of Vulcan B2, XH557. He
then went to RAF Akrotiri, Cyprus,
where he served as Crew Chief
on Vulcan B2, XJ781. In 1974 he
left the service and joined Amoco,
where he was installation manager
working on North Sea oil rigs. He
currently runs the Vulcan Crew
Chief Register, which aims to
assist ex-Vulcan crew chiefs keep
in contact with each other.

**OPPOSITE An Avro Vulcan B2 of No 617 Squadron at RAF
Scampton is prepared for a sortie during August 1963.** *IWM
RAF T4135*

**ABOVE Crew Chief
Tony Regan 'out East'.**
Tony Regan

Pre-flight inspection

When I came on shift, the first thing I did was to check the display board in the Technical Operations Room, to establish whether my aircraft was scheduled to fly that day. If it was, I would note the take off time and the fuel load required. I would then look through the Form 700E and the job cards, to check that the faults from the last flight had been rectified. I would also check the Form 700E, to see whether any out-of-phase servicing was required.

Normally the starter crew comprised me and three technicians, an airframe man, an engine man and an electrician. When we drove out to the aircraft we brought the necessary documentation and towed a Palouste turbine engine starting rig, a Houchin 200 Volt 400-cycle electrical power rig, and a hydraulic platform or a set of steps. When we arrived at the aircraft we carried out an external inspection, looking carefully for any signs of damage. It was not unknown, in the small hours of the morning, for some half-asleep bod driving a truck to clip an aircraft without being aware of it.

The technicians then carried out their pre-flights. The airframe fitter inspected the airframe including the tyres, the brake assemblies and the undercarriage. He also checked the pressure in the nitrogen, oxygen, the low pressure air systems and the engine rapid start air system (if fitted), and topped up these as necessary. His schedule was also included cleaning the crews' windows, and conducting a visual inspection of the top surface of the wings.

Refuelling

Normally we used two refuelling tankers, one positioned front of each wing, with their refuelling pipes connected to the fuel charging point in each main wheel undercarriage bay. The required percentage fuel load was then set on the refuelling control unit, in the port undercarriage bay. During the refuelling operation the engine man sat in the cockpit, keeping a careful watch on the fuel gauges and the centre-of-gravity indicator. It was important to ensure that the fuel tanks were filled in the correct sequence, Nos 1, 4, 5 and 7 on each side, then Nos 2, 3 and 6, so the aircraft did not become tail-heavy. If things did not look right, fuel would be transferred from the No 7 tanks (those furthest to the rear) to the No 1 tanks (those furthest forward).

The engine man checked the oil level of each engine and that at each constant speed drive unit. He also looked for signs of an oil leak, and checked the air intakes and the inlet guide vanes of each engine. At the rear he checked each jet pipe for security, and for signs that anything unusual had passed through an engine.

Once the refuelling operation was complete, the 200V AC supply was connected to the aircraft. If the aircraft had not flown for some time, I would switch on the electrically powered flying control units, to check that the system warning lights went out when the units were running properly. I would also test the functioning of the controls, moving the control stick and the rudder pedals to their full travel each way, and making sure that the control surfaces gave the correct indications on the control surface indicator on the pilots' instrument panel.

ABOVE LEFT
Refuelling and servicing an 83 Squadron Vulcan at RAF Scampton in 1963. *IWM RAF T4833*

ABOVE Engine start for an 83 Squadron Vulcan. *IWM RAF T5070*

LEFT AND FAR LEFT
Refuelling XH558.
Vulcan to the Sky Trust

Crew Chief checks

Before anyone else entered the aircraft, I would check that the ejection seats had the safety pins in position. In addition I would inspect the piping to the pilots' and the rear crew's personal equipment connectors, and also the rear crew's parachutes. My final item in the internal inspection was to ensure there were no loose objects in the cabin. I then left the aircraft, and thereafter nobody was allowed to enter the aircraft apart from myself or the flight crew. I then did a final walk round inspection, as laid down in the servicing schedule.

The pre-flight check on the Vulcan was normally straightforward. When the flight crew arrived, I would review the Form 700E with the captain. We both signed the flight servicing sheet, the Form 700E would fly with the aircraft.

Meanwhile, the starter crew removed the undercarriage locks. I would show these, and the pitot and static vent covers, to the AEO before storing them in the tool box in the cabin. I would assist the pilots to strap in, and withdraw the safety pins to make the ejection seats and the canopy live. I would pass the safety pins to the pilots, to place in the stowages below the cockpit coaming.

I then exited the aircraft, and plugged my intercom lead into the socket in the nose wheel bay. That allowed me to communicate with the flight crew as they went through their check list. It seemed to me that some crews took a lot longer to do this than others – particularly if it was blowing half a gale and raining hard! When the captain checked the flying controls and the air brakes, I would confirm their correct functioning. Then the control surfaces were set for take-off.

If we were using the Palouste to start the engines, the captain would now ask me to start the rig. When it was running properly, he

ABOVE **The crew chief hands over the aircraft to the pilot, who signs the Form 700E.** *IWM RAF T4837*

BELOW **Ready to go.** *Jonathan Falconer collection*

checked with me that all was clear behind the aircraft. Then he started an engine, usually the No 4. Once it reached 90 per cent rpm, he cross fed air from that engine to start the remaining three engines in turn. The Palouste was then stopped and removed. When the main alternators were running properly and switched on line, the power unit was shut down and removed. Alternatively, if the rapid start system was fitted, the pilot might use it to start the No 4 engine, and then cross fed air to start the other three. When all four engines were running, the pilot tested the bomb doors and the air brakes, and I confirmed their correct operation. I then handed the marshalling to the ground crew, and the aircraft taxied out.

Post-flight inspection

When the aircraft was returning to base, Technical Operations would inform me. With the ground crew I would go out to the pan and make sure all items of equipment were in the safe area behind the white lines. I would have two men in position to marshal the aircraft on to the pan, and stop it about 20ft from the final position. Then I would take-over. I would plug in my intercom lead, and talk the captain

on to the hooking point. Then we could tie the nose wheel down to a strong point (necessary if high winds or snow conditions were forecast).

I then opened the entrance door, climbed in and made safe the pilots' ejection seats and the canopy. Meanwhile, the ground crew placed the chocks in position so the pilot could shut down the engines and release the brakes.

I would accompany the flight crew to the technical debrief, to discuss any unserviceable items. The ground crew trade managers were present at the debriefing to discuss any issues with the crew. Then the Form 700E was annotated with the faults, so I could raise the relevant job cards. The flying crew then departed to Flying Operations.

I would enter the flying time in the Form 700E, when advised by Operations. If any out-of-phase servicing was required, I would raise the job cards for these. The after-flight inspection would begin with checks by the various specialists. The engine air inlets and inlet guide vanes would be examined in detail, looking for damage and possible bird strikes. Also the jet pipes would be inspected carefully, looking for cracks and damage.

Once the tyres and brakes had cooled down sufficiently after landing, these would be inspected for damage and flats, and for any signs of leaking hydraulic oil, lubricating oil or fuel. Then we would replenish the compressed air, oxygen and oil systems. At this stage the aircraft would normally be refuelled to 70 per cent, unless directed otherwise.

If the tail brake parachute had been deployed, and there was sufficient daylight, a packed parachute would be fitted in its place. Unless there was an urgent operational reason, this operation was not attempted in the dark. Refitting a brake parachute in poor light was considered a dangerous operation, which carried the risk that a ground crewman might fall off the lift on to the concrete below.

The pitot head covers, static vent plugs and engine blanks would be refitted. Then I would make a last minute check inside the aircraft, close the entrance door and earth the aircraft (to prevent any build-up of static electricity). Finally, I would take the documentation to the Crew Chiefs' office, where it was held ready for the next flight.

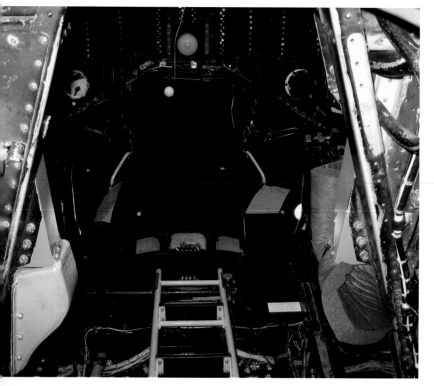

BELOW The crew chief's view of the Vulcan cockpit, looking up through the floor hatch into the crew compartment.
Vulcan to the Sky Trust

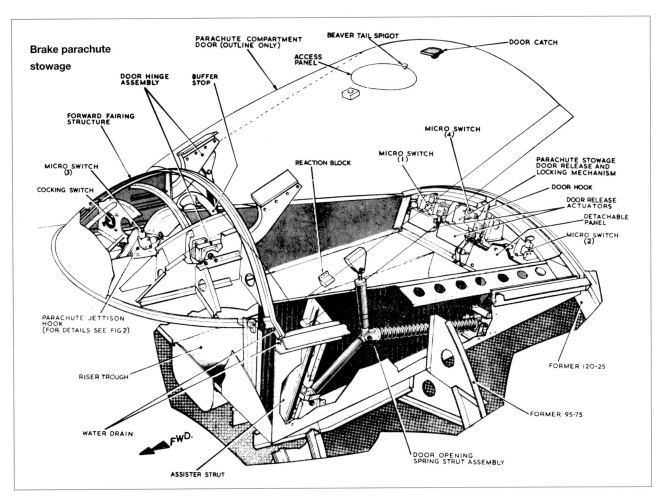

Brake parachute
stowage

PARACHUTE COMPARTMENT
DOOR (OUTLINE ONLY)

BEAVER TAIL SPIGOT

DOOR CATCH

ACCESS
PANEL

DOOR HINGE
ASSEMBLY

BUFFER
STOP

FORWARD FAIRING
STRUCTURE

MICRO SWITCH
(4)

MICRO SWITCH
(1)

PARACHUTE STOWAGE
DOOR RELEASE AND
LOCKING MECHANISM

REACTION BLOCK

MICRO SWITCH
(3)

COCKING SWITCH

DOOR HOOK

DOOR RELEASE
ACTUATORS

DETACHABLE
PANEL

MICRO SWITCH
(2)

PARACHUTE JETTISON
HOOK
(FOR DETAILS SEE FIG.2)

FORMER 120·25

RISER TROUGH

FORMER 95·75

WATER DRAIN

FWD.

DOOR OPENING
SPRING STRUT ASSEMBLY

ASSISTER STRUT

ABOVE Brake parachue stowage.

LEFT Tail parachute being fitted to 83 Squadron Vulcan at RAF Scampton in 1963. Normally when working from a long runway the Vulcan does not need to stream its brake parachute. When packed in its bag the parachute weighs about 200lb, and when it is streamed the parachute has a diameter of 45ft. The door of the brake parachute compartment is operated by powerful springs, and personnel were told to exercise extreme caution working near the brake parachute door. Particular care is required during the fitting and removal operations and, except in an operational emergency, no attempt should be made to fit the brake parachute in the dark. Some technicians suffered serious injuries when they lost their footing and fell onto the concrete hard standing beneath the aircraft. *IWM RAF T5064*

RIGHT Tail parachute being fitted to XH558. *Vulcan to the Sky Trust*

Chapter 8

Vulcan to the Sky

The restoration of Vulcan B2, XH558, to flying status was always considered to be a highly ambitious and challenging project. And so it would prove to be. This aspect of the story began in March 1984 when the last Vulcan squadron disbanded. However, the RAF decided to maintain two B2s, XL426 and XH558, in flying condition. Manned by RAF volunteers of the Vulcan Display Flight, XL426 continued to delight crowds at air shows during the next three air display seasons. At the end of the 1986 season this aircraft went into honourable retirement. In its place came XH558, which continued in that role until the autumn of 1992, when it too had nearly run out of flying hours.

OPPOSITE XH558 takes off at the Farnborough Air Show in 2008. *Vulcan to the Sky Trust*

Under pressure from the Treasury, the Ministry of Defence announced that it was unable to allocate funds for the major overhaul of what was, after all, an obsolete if venerable aircraft. The Ministry therefore decided to put up the Vulcan for disposal. Her fate was to be determined by an auction using sealed bids.

David Walton, a director of C. Walton Ltd, which owned Bruntingthorpe airfield near Leicester, later described his first encounter with the aircraft:

'The Ministry of Defence had decided that this most famous of all post-war aircraft should be put up for disposal. Without any prompting, tender papers duly arrived in the post. An appointment was made with RAF Waddington for us to view the aircraft and when we arrived we were shown around by a somewhat disconsolate ground crew member. XH558 looked immaculate, standing proudly in her hangar being worked upon by the service crew. The bomb bay doors displaying the word "FAREWELL" said it all. We were told that a petition "Save the Vulcan" with over 200,000 signatures had been submitted to Parliament, but all to no avail. The service crew told us of the prospective purchasers who had been to view her and of some of their plans for her, including an anonymous group who proposed to disembowel her and turn her into a restaurant – presumably the chef's special would have been "Bomb Bay Duck"!'

Into private hands

David Walton decided that this threatened desecration of a national icon could not be permitted. Fortunately he had the will – and more importantly the means – to prevent it. He submitted a tender offering £25,000 for the aircraft plus 800 tons of spare parts and a mass of servicing documents and other relevant papers. After a nail-biting wait, in March 1993 the Ministry of Defence announced its acceptance of Walton's bid. Under the terms of the sale an RAF crew delivered the aircraft to Bruntingthorpe airfield, which was to be its new home. In its current state XH558 was no longer permitted to fly until it had undergone a full overhaul. But its proud owners maintained it in

condition to taxi under its own power.

At this time Andrew Edmondson had his first contact with XH558. Andrew's service career had included six months as a line servicing mechanic working on Vulcans, before he went on to Phantoms and Tornados. After being invalided out of the RAF he had taken a job managing one of with Age Concern's furniture shops. One day a customer mentioned the Vulcan at Bruntingthorpe, and Andrew's ears pricked up. He recalled: 'In September 1993 I went to the airfield and met Terry Smith, a licensed engineer brought in by C. Walton Ltd to look after the Vulcan. The company's aspirations for the aeroplane were very focussed: they wanted to fly it. They were advised to look after it and keep it in the condition in which they had received it, to help it meet the certification requirements to fly. I joined a small team of unpaid volunteers that worked on the Vulcan on weekends.'

Being focussed was all well and good, but David Walton was under no illusions regarding the huge amount of money – probably running into seven figures – required to return the aircraft to flight.

In the meantime, the Vulcan continued its air display career in a more limited fashion. In the summer of 1994 Bruntingthorpe held its first 'Big Thunder' air display, at which XH558 marked the high point. The bomber fired up its engines and taxied to one end of the runway. Then it began a full power run, accelerating rapidly and noisily. As it neared the middle of the runway, the pilot pulled back the throttles and raised the nose to achieve maximum aerodynamic braking. Then, as the aircraft slowed, he lowered the nose wheel firmly on the runway and deployed the huge braking parachute. The aircraft came to a spectacular halt, then taxied in clear of the runway. The pilot released the brake parachute, and taxied back to its hard standing. And that was the end of its show. The pilot was not permitted to lift the main wheels off the ground, and at the time most people believed that it would never fly again.

Also in 1994 David Thorpe, an ex-Vulcan crew chief, joined the team working on the Vulcan. During the next couple of years he carefully instructed Andrew Edmondson on the aircraft and its systems. At the end of that time Andrew was appointed as crew chief of the Bruntingthorpe Vulcan.

The 'Big Thunder' air display became an annual event in the late 1990s. At the same time the collection of pensioned off military aircraft at the airfield had expanded, and now included a Handley Page Victor, a Blackburn Buccaneer a Hawker Hunter and other types.

A chance encounter

Within its limits the Vulcan displays were dramatic, but some people felt the bomber could do much, much, better than that. One such was Dr Robert Pleming, holder of a PhD in nuclear physics and Technical Director of Cisco Systems, the world's largest networking company. On top of that he held impressive credentials in industry and a wide range of contacts. Later he commented: 'My relationship with Vulcan began in the mid-1980s, when I saw it performing at air shows. I thought it was the most spectacular aircraft on the air show circuit, a real treat to watch. I joined the restoration group, and one day I saw David Walton on the airfield. We had not been introduced but I knew what he looked like, so I went up to him and said "Hello", then I asked him what plans he had for the Vulcan.'

Walton replied that he had been in contact with the Civil Aviation Authority concerning the granting of permission to fly the aircraft at air shows, but as things stood they were not particularly helpful. With Walton's agreement, Pleming said he would use his wide range of contacts to see if a better structured application might be possible. Robert Pleming again: 'That chance encounter turned out to be absolutely vital for the future of the Vulcan. If I hadn't struck up that conversation, we wouldn't have a Vulcan flying today.'

As a first step, during 1997 a small team of experts came together to consider whether it was technically feasible to restore XH558 to flight. Named The Vulcan Operating Company (TVOC), the team comprised Pleming himself as leader, David Walton, Vulcan pilot David Thomas, Vulcan Crew chief David Thorpe, one-time chief designer at BAe Systems Peter Beushaw, and ex-RAF engineering officer

Earl Pick. Also, to cover the political flank, ex-Member of Parliament and ex-RAF Vulcan pilot Keith Mans joined the team.

To back this move, C. Walton Ltd purchased the entire inventory of Vulcan spare parts held at the RAF Maintenance Unit at Stafford. These items were all specific to the Vulcan and were, therefore, useless for any other aircraft type. Their commercial value was limited to their weight as scrap metal. For an outlay of £130,000 the company obtained a veritable treasure trove. The haul included seven Olympus turbojet engines, eight airborne auxiliary power plants, six jet pipes, four cockpit canopies, two fins, three front doors as well as several thousand smaller items. Most of these items were brand new and still in their original protective wrappings. It required forty-eight lorry loads, each with a 40ft long commercial container, to shift the haul to Bruntingthorpe.

Amassing support

Late in 1997 Pleming and Walton met representatives from the Civil Aviation Authority (CAA), to discuss the administrative hurdles they needed to cross in order to fly the Vulcan and display it at air shows. The CAA's primary requirement was that British Aerospace (BAe) Systems – as inheritor of the old A.V. Roe Company – had to agree to serve as the design authority.

During the next year or so Robert Pleming devoted his considerable management expertise to securing high level industrial and

CAA support for the project. The board of BAe Systems gave its encouragement, and provided the all-important paperwork to obtain a type design approval. Also the company's one time chief designer, Peter Beushaw, became an avid supporter of the project and gave much invaluable advice.

In May 1999 BAe Systems formally agreed to continue to act as design authority for the restoration to flight of the reconstructed Vulcan. Since TVOC lacked the capability to manage the reconstruction on its own, and BAe Systems could not spare its employees to do so, it was agreed to bring Marshall Aerospace at Cambridge into the project to serve as the engineering authority and technical design authority.

In 1999 Andrew Edmondson was appointed engineering manager for the project, and became a full time employee of C. Walton Ltd. Now one of his main tasks, assisted by a team of volunteers, was to identify the current status of the manufacturer of each individual part of the aircraft. These companies held the proprietary rights – the copyright of the design if you will – to manufacture or repair these items. The identification process was easy enough

if those companies were still trading. For example, Dunlop had made the braking system. Boulton Paul had made the powered flying control units. Dowty (now Messier-Dowty) had built the undercarriage. Lucas had made the electrical components (before it was bought out by TRW in the United States, which in turn sold it to B.F. Goodrich).

As might be expected, the most difficult companies to track down were those that manufactured the smallest parts of the aircraft. Andrew Edmondson explained: 'Teddington Seals in Merthyr Tydfil had produced the nylon diaphragms for the fuel pressurisation system. Nylon dries out, so we needed to get replacements for those seals. But it took a lot of detective work to find Teddington, they had been bought out many years earlier. And the companies that bought bits of the company had sold out also. It took more than two years of hunting, before we eventually traced the guy who held the design rights to manufacture those seals.'

At the same time, the team carried out a detailed technical survey of the aircraft, to assess the amount of engineering work necessary to return it to flight. The team determined that the project was feasible, and went on to carry out a more detailed technical survey which it completed in February 2000.

Enter the Heritage Lottery Fund

Now the stage was set for the most daunting task of all: that of raising the formidable sum of money needed to finance the project. C. Walton Ltd had generously contributed its own company funds to lay the foundations for the restoration project, it could do no more.

The most likely source of money to pay for the restoration was the Heritage Lottery Fund. Armed with the promise of support from the CAA and BAe Systems, Robert Pleming and Felicity Irwin, the head fund raiser, began work on a bid for a grant from the Lottery Fund. But before that could happen, it was necessary to change the business model for the project. The Lottery Fund does not accept bids from limited companies, the bidders had to be registered charitable trusts. To solve that problem the assets of TVOC were passed to the Vulcan to the Sky Trust (VTST), a registered charitable trust which would control the project from now on. Air Chief Marshal Sir Michael Knight agreed to accept the post of chairman of the trust, and became the public face of the project.

The team also learned that, that as a matter of policy, the Lottery Fund does not support organisations aiming to restore an historic aircraft to flight. Andrew Edmondson described the semantic stratagem the team used to by-pass that particular difficulty. 'The team discovered that the Fund had provided money for the overhaul of a Second World War German tank, to restore it to "full working order". So we said we wanted only to restore the Vulcan to "full working order". We said we did not want a full flying aeroplane, just one that had been restored to the point where, when it reached 136mph, it could take off. But at that point the grant would finish.'

This was tongue-in-cheek verbal juggling of a high order but, hey, what did they have to lose? In the event that initial request for Lottery funding failed, and in December 2002 VTST issued a press release announcing its

disappointment. At about that time the tabloid press was running a series of campaigns lambasting some of the lottery grants it considered to be 'a waste of public money'. In contrast, the newspapers were almost unanimous in supporting the refurbishment of the Vulcan as a worthwhile project for the Fund to support. Readers were invited to write to the Lottery Fund to make their views known. Andrew Edmondson again:

'That stimulated a lot of press coverage, and also gained for us quite a bit of parliamentary and industry support. The Lottery Fund was inundated with e-mails complaining about the rejection. At one point they had seventeen thousand e-mails clogging up their system. The Fund's lawyers wrote and told us to stop sending all those complaining e-mails. We replied – truthfully – that the e-mails had not come from us, they had come from the public'.

The episode had been a bruising experience for the Lottery Fund, but there was a positive outcome so far as VTST was concerned. The Lottery Fund's representatives now agreed to talk to VTST, to discuss the weaknesses of the original bid and suggest ways in which it could be improved.

ABOVE If you can't find it, you don't own it. The storage facility at Bruntingthorpe for Vulcan spare parts contained 32,000 items, all of them carefully catalogued. The Vulcan Technical Library has a 1,500-volume Vulcan technical archive purchased from the RAF.

It turned out that the rejection of the original bid had nothing at all to do with the definition of 'full working order'. The issue did not even hinge on the engineering plan, which the Lottery Trustees had accepted. The problem was that in its current form the proposal gave insufficient emphasis on the educational value of the project. The bidders were advised to lay stress on the Vulcan's role in the Cold War, a subject that formed part of the state schools' history curriculum. VTST was also advised to emphasise the Vulcan's excellence as a piece of engineering, which in its time had been at the forefront of aircraft design.

It took several iterations of the draft proposal, and some detailed discussions, before the wording of the next bid was agreed. In order to place the required 'tick' in the education box, VTST agreed to establish a post for a full time paid history teacher, to organise properly structured visits to see the Vulcan to learn about it. Also, to fit in with the new arrangement, VTST agreed to purchase the Vulcan and the large collection of spare parts from C. Walton Ltd, for the sum of £125,000.

Lottery success

The outcome of the second bid fully justified the effort involved in its preparation. Lodged in 2003, in the summer of the following year it secured an award of just over £2.7 million. Together with around £900,000 raised from donations from the public and fund raising events, that would allow the restoration work on XH558 to commence in 2005. After years of scrimping and begging, the project at last appeared to have a firm financial footing. Andrew Edmondson summed up the team's mood:

'Once the Lottery Fund came on board with a grant, this gave substance to a dream. Remember, until then the four of us had been working in a breezy old hangar in the wilds of Leicestershire. We were your typical British eccentrics, a bunch of enthusiasts who wanted to see the aeroplane fly. We told anyone who would listen: "We are enthusiastic, but we are not enthusiasts. We are professional people and we believe that with our skills we would be able to put this aeroplane into the air."'

The CAA had no policy reason for denying the Vulcan a Permit to Fly. Nevertheless, the path to obtaining that all-important document would prove long and arduous. The complex bomber was widely different from the normal run of aircraft types for which the Authority issued such permits. The requirements of a modern bureaucracy did not fit comfortably astride a military aircraft that was nearly half a century old, and which had not met those conditions in the first place.

When the restoration work began, the first move was to strip down the airframe and inspect the components in minute detail. In particular, the team needed to establish the amount of decay, corrosion and general deterioration that had taken place during the previous decades. This was no easy task, for a visual inspection of the structure could get only so far. The technicians removed the various access panels and crawled all over the airframe. But there remained large areas of internal structure that were inaccessible in the normal way. These were checked using non-destructive methods employing X-rays, eddy currents, boroscope and ultrasound techniques.

Replacing the damaged parts was not always a straightforward business, especially in those cases where the materials used in constructing the original item were no longer available. That was the case with some types of nuts and bolts that were no longer being manufactured. Where the original materials were no longer available, substitutes had to be used. Yet, even when a modern substitute material had superior characteristics to the original, it still had to undergo a lengthy process to gain design approval before it could be cleared for use.

There was however one useful source for items that were no longer available using the normal channels. More than a dozen Vulcans, some complete and others less so, were sitting on the ground at the various aviation museums and collections. These aircraft would never fly again. The team at Bruntingthorpe made good use of the engineering technique known as 'Christmas Treeing': obtaining parts taken from other Vulcans, though always with their owners' consent.

Financial problems

The work of restoring XH558 was well advanced by August 2006, when a financial crisis came close to bringing the project to an untimely end. The dream was in danger of turning into a nightmare. The core of the problem was that areas of corrosion were found in several places, and it cost both Marshall Aerospace and VTTS TVOC much more than expected to put it right. To take just one example, the elevons and rudder on XH558 were found to have suffered corrosion. This was worse on the inboard elevons but could be repaired on the outboard's surfaces. The work to restore a set of eight elevons and a rudder, undertaken by Beagle Aerospace at Christchurch, cost £225,000. In this and other areas, VTTS funds started to drain away rapidly. If matters continued in that way for much longer, the money was likely to run out long before the aircraft was ready to fly.

With their collective backs to the wall, the Vulcan to the Skies team and its cohort of willing helpers went into emergency fund raising mode. A well publicised appeal raised over £700,000. It was a magnificent effort, but it was not quite enough. Then, at the last moment, Sir Jack Hayward made a generous donation of £500,000. For a while longer the project was safe.

It never rains but it pours. Work on the project had just resumed when there was an ominous discovery. Inside each wing there were areas of corrosion much more difficult to reach than those found earlier, caused by the ingress of moisture over a long period. To reach those areas it was necessary to remove almost the entire skinning on the upper surface of each wing, and roll it to one side. The task had to be performed with the utmost care because any damaged skins could not be replaced – such large areas of light alloy were no longer being manufactured.

ABOVE **Roll-out in 2006.** *Vulcan to the Sky Trust*

BELOW **Checking the high energy ignition units at the front of the engine.** *Vulcan to the Sky Trust*

A massive job

Opening up the structure was a gargantuan task, involving the removal of around 25,000 rivets on each side of the aircraft. That amount of work was way beyond the resources of VTST, and the trustees were forced to bring in a team of specialised riveters to do the work. At one point there were a dozen riveters, six on each wing, working eighteen hours a day. Andrew Edmondson recalled:

'It was a massive job, and one that we had not expected. Rolling back the skins exposed the J-section beams and stringers that supported the structure of the wings. Once it was possible to get to the top and bottom of each area of corrosion, the affected areas could be polished down to the good metal. Either that, or we would cut out the corroded beams and splice in new ones. It was all close-tolerance work.

'The task of removing the corrosion introduced a three-month delay in the restoration work. That meant that instead of starting the engine runs in July 2007, as planned, they began in October. As a result we missed the 2007 air display

season, which was disappointing for everybody. And it gobbled up the £500,000 in the budget earmarked to cover contingencies.'

When the bomber was reassembled, many strictly military systems were deactivated and returned to the bomber. These boxes still had a useful role to play, serving as ballast to restore the bomber's centre of gravity to its proper place. Examples of this were the bombing radar and its associated computers, and various electronic countermeasures systems.

First flight post-restoration

On 18 October 2007 the bomber made its long awaited first post-restoration flight. It lasted 34 minutes and went off without a hitch. The Vulcan was almost ready to strut its stuff at air shows, but by then the 2007 display season was over. The aircraft spent the winter in the hangar at Bruntingthorpe.

The Vulcan emerged from its winter hibernation on 14 April 2008, to make another

test flight before landing at RAF Cottesmore to have the compasses swung. While it was airborne a fire warning light illuminated on the control panel of the airborne auxiliary power plant. The crew declared a full Mayday emergency and landed at Cottesmore. Once down, it was found that the cause was a false warning due to an electrical fault.

Two days later XH558 again took off, for a test flight planned to last two hours. However, this flight had also to be abandoned, when a main wheel undercarriage door failed to close on retraction. This time the problem was a malfunctioning electrical microswitch.

During the next couple of months the Vulcan underwent further flight testing. Then, on 3 July 2008, the aircraft at last received its Permit to Fly from the CAA. That afternoon it flew to RAF Waddington, where it demonstrated its air display routine in front of the Authority's officials. That display gained a Display Authorisation, the final all-important piece of paper allowing it to display before the public.

On 5 July, at Waddington, XH558 made its first public air display following its restoration. It went off without a hitch. First there was a fly past in company with the Avro Lancaster of the Battle of Britain Memorial Flight, then the Vulcan delivered its planned solo display to an enthusiastic crowd.

As a display aircraft the Vulcan XH558 is restricted to a maximum speed of 250kts, or

ABOVE Ready to roll.

Ian Waudby

BELOW XH558's first flight crew. From left: David Thomas, Barry Masefield and Al McDicken. David flew 558 out of service in 1993 and then back into the air again in 1997. He is the Vulcan Display Pilot and was VTST Chief Pilot during 558's flight-testing programme. *Vulcan to the Sky Trust*

300kts if, as would happen from time to time, it flew in formation with the Hawk aircraft of The Red Arrows. It is limited to a maximum altitude of 17,500ft, and is restricted to flight only in clear weather daytime conditions, following visual flight rules. To conserve engine life, the Vulcan is limited to a maximum of 50 flying hours per year.

For the rest of the 2008 air display season, it was a case of good news and bad news. Andrew Edmondson reviewed the aircraft's performance during that period: 'Out of the twenty-four air displays we planned during the 2008 display season, we flew fourteen. Eight of those were lost for technical reasons, and four were lost to poor weather. Most of the technical problems were teething troubles. Remember, we had not been able to do any shakedown flights. The Vulcan had done just six hours of flying, and that was it. So we knew we were going to have teething problems. The only major problem we had was from a door bracket which sheered during a display at Brize Norton. We replaced the bracket and there has been no problem since.'

New financial crisis

At the beginning of 2009 the project ran into yet another financial crisis. The credit crunch had taken a hefty bite from the value of many people's share portfolios, and the hoped-for wealthy sponsor had failed to materialise. Robert Pleming described the 'perfect storm' he now faced.

'Up to the end of the 2008 display season, the assumption in our business plan had been that we would gain a major commercial sponsor who would meet most of the costs of flying the aircraft. In the event, with the recession and the resultant massive shrinkage in marketing budgets, the idea of gaining a sponsorship went out of the window. And much as my public face said "We are going to fly the Vulcan again at air shows", my head said "Oh, geez, this may be the end for it."'

Yet again it was necessary to mount a campaign to assemble support from the public. This time the call was for 20,000 donors willing to pledge £4 per month to save the project, aiming at a target of £1 million. The proposed regular monthly payment would be more valuable to the project than even quite a large one-off payment, since the former would create a dependable revenue stream. Thanks to powerful support from *The Mail on Sunday*, the pledges reached the target figure of £1 million early in March 2009.

With that as a launch pad, the Vulcan had a hugely successful display season in 2009. The aircraft had been booked to make thirty-seven displays or fly-bys. Three events had to be cancelled for technical reasons, and two more fell foul of bad weather. But the other thirty-two events went ahead as planned. Following its last display flight on 26 September 2009, XH558 went into the hangar at RAF Lyneham for its winter hibernation.

The Vulcan has demonstrated that it

has what the advertising people call 'Brand Recognition', and it has it in spades. Those air displays whose programmes included the aircraft have enjoyed significantly larger attendance figures than in previous years. Another, less scientific, measure of the aircraft's appeal is the speed with which the beer tent empties following the announcement that the Vulcan is about to strut its stuff.

Be that as it may, at the beginning of 2010 the financial position was once again becoming difficult. Then, at the end of February 2010, the project received another unexpected shot in the arm, this time in the shape of a bequest for £458,000 from an anonymous donor. Together with the money raised from other sources and pledges, VTTS found itself in a better financial position than it had enjoyed for some time.

Let the last word on the subject go to the man who, more than any other, deserves credit for his efforts to restore the Vulcan to flight: Dr Robert Pleming.

'Had I known I was going to spend nigh on ten years of my life on the Vulcan to the Skies project, I would probably not have set out on that route. But the problem is, once you have started out on a thing like that, you cannot just stop. It became a matter of integrity, people were depending on me. They hoped to see the Vulcan fly again and I was honour-bound to do my very best to achieve that goal.'

Amen to that.

Chapter 9

The Restoration of Vulcan XH558

The chapter that follows will allow the reader can gain an impression of the sheer technical complexity of the Vulcan and the enormous amount of painstaking work that was necessary to restore the aircraft to flight. Every moveable component had to be removed from the aircraft and carefully inspected and then, if possible, it would be renovated and returned to the aircraft, or else replaced. It was indeed a labour-intensive effort.

OPPOSITE XH558 inside the hangar at Bruntingthorpe.

All photos in this chapter are © Vulcan to the Sky Trust except where credited otherwise.

135

INSTALLATION OF POWERED FLYING CONTROL SURFACES

The elevons, by virtue of their size, are awkward items to move into position on the wings. A specially designed lifting strop is therefore necessary, which fits between the crane hook and the elevon, to support the latter as it is pushed into place. The rudder also has its own specially designed lifting strop, to hold it in the near-vertical position as it is moved into position.

1 Some of the magnesium alloy-covered control surfaces had suffered corrosion damage and needed to be sent to Beagle Aerospace at Christchurch, Hants, for refurbishment.

2 An elevon undergoes refurbishment, showing the internal structure.

3 An inboard elevon with the skin removed, revealing the internal structure.

4 Refurbishment complete, the elevon awaits re-skinning.

5 The powered flying control units (PFC units) hang down from their main brackets before they are connected to the elevons.

6 A close-up of a PFC unit fitted with its electric motor, awaiting attachment to the control surface. This small unit (2ft 6in long, about the height of a traffic cone) has a big job to do in overcoming aerodynamic forces to control the aircraft.

7 The arrival of the refurbished elevons at Bruntingthorpe.

8 Preparing the wing to receive the elevon.

9 One of the port outboard elevons being lifted into position for attachment to the aircraft. Once the elevon has been fitted, the fairing on the underside of the wing will be closed to protect the aerodynamic seal and the PFC units. Ron Evans (on top of the wing) can be seen guiding the elevon into position.

10 The installation of the starboard outboard elevon. David Fisher is guiding the trailing edge of the control surface into place, assisted by Ron Evans in the white overalls. The elevon hangs from the lifting strop (in the centre of the photograph), which itself hangs from the hook of the mobile crane.

11 Port outboard elevon being fitted.

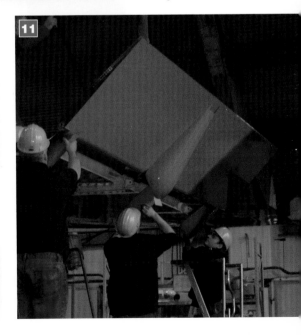

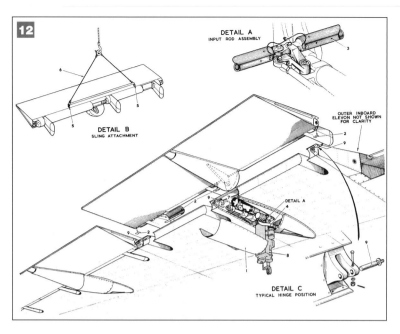

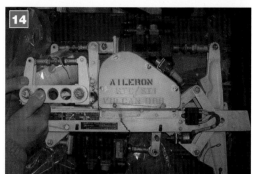

12 Procedure for removal of outboard elevons.

13 David Fisher taps home the fulcrum pin to locate one of the elevons in its housing.

14 The hand on the left of the picture gives scale to the aileron artificial feel unit located on the starboard side of the bomb bay. In this unit the 'feel' is provided by the effort required to twist two torsion bars. That effort remains constant, whatever the airspeed. However, the amount of control surface movement available to execute banking manoeuvres is progressively reduced as the airspeed increases. The elevator artificial feel box is similar in size and is located on the port side of the bomb bay.

15 Installation of the rudder. The aircraft is ready to receive the rudder, with the port side access door in the fin in the open position.

16 Hoisting the rudder into position, with Nick Clarke and Ron Evans waiting to receive and locate the control surface.

17 The rudder is finally in position, with the aerodynamic fairing open.

ENGINE INSTALLATION

Engine removal (or refitting) requires a team of six technicians, comprising the team leader, the second-in-command and four men to operate the Didsbury hand winches. When the four winches and their operators are in place and ready to take the weight of the engine, the team leader and the second-in-command remove the three locking pins that hold the engine in place. The team leader then directs the operation to lower the engine, while the second-in-command watches from the air intake bay to ensure that the engine remains square with the locating channels. Once the relevant disconnections (or connections) have been made it takes about 3 hours to get an engine out of (or into) the aircraft.

1 The view from the rear of the aircraft, with the two starboard engine access doors open.

2 Engine removal (three-point hoisting).

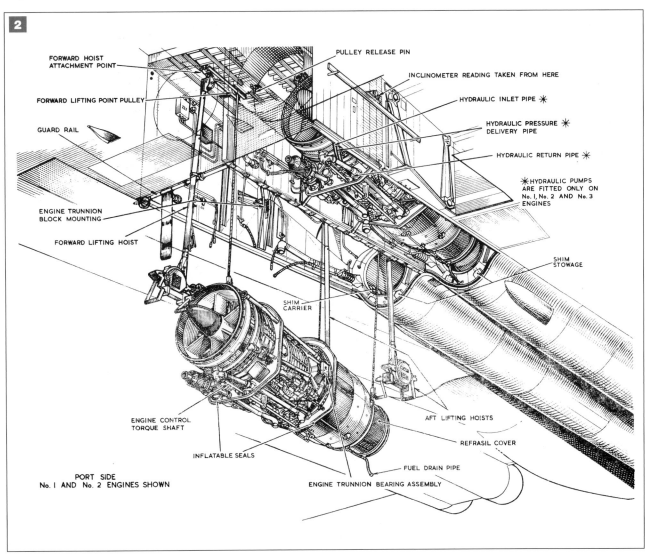

3 One of the starboard engines is lowered from its housing using four yellow-painted Didsbury hand hoists.

4 Slowly the Olympus is lowered from the engine bay.

5 Having been removed from the aircraft, the engine now sits on its transportation stand.

6 A Jetcel environmental protection bag houses an Olympus engine that has been brought out of storage.

7 The engine is removed from the Jetcel bag.

8 John Boyle carries out an inspection of an Olympus engine before it is installed in the aircraft.

9 Derek Marshal inspects the installation of one of the main alternators (at the top of the photo) fitted to its constant speed drive unit (the unit Derek is touching). Each of these units generates a maximum of 40 KVA, and the photo shows the small size of the components of this highly efficient system.

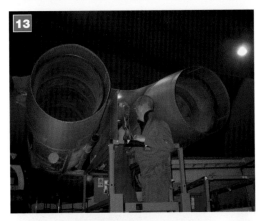

10 Preparing to install the jet pipe of the No 3 engine.

11 Slowly the jet pipe is edged into place.

12 and 13 Repairs are carried out to the internal skins of the jet pipe tunnel for No 4 engine.

14 Olympus fully installed.

15 Steve Hands uses a detergent to degrease the air intakes prior to priming and then painting.

EMERGENCY ELECTRICAL POWER

1 In addition to the four Olympus engines the Vulcan B2 carried a fifth engine, the Rover BF Goodrich AAPP. This small turbojet engine produced electrical power for ground or emergency use, as well as compressed air for engine starting. It is seen on the right, mounted upside-down, on top of its special test rig. Malcolm Lawrence is carrying out the test and overhaul. Note that the engine exhaust, on the extreme right, is pointing upwards. Had the exhaust been pointing downwards, it might have lifted the test rig off the ground. The blue-painted items in the picture belong to the test rig; the green tubes are part of the carrying frame for the AAPP.

Since the Vulcan B2 has no manual back-up for its powered flying control systems, its designers adopted a 'belt, braces and jock-strap' approach to electrical power generation. As well as four large engine-driven alternators (any one of which generates enough power to keep the aircraft in the air), there is the Airborne Auxiliary Power Plant (for use at low altitudes) or the ram air turbine (for use at high altitudes). Thus the aircraft can continue flying provided just one out of its five separate alternator systems is working fully.

2, 3 and 4 The AAPP, right way up and in its own self contained fire-proof box, is hoisted into position in the aircraft.

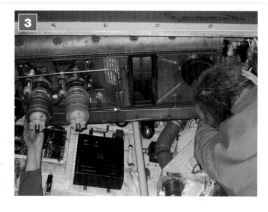

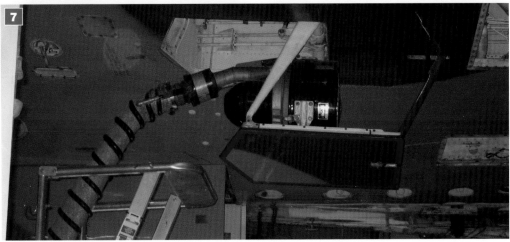

5 Nick Clarke connects the main bracket to the Ram Air Turbine (RAT) before installing it on its platform beneath the port wing.

6 Sam Evans gives scale to the RAT installation. Once this device is lowered into position under the port wing, and provided the aircraft's speed is not less than 250kts (indicated) at altitudes above 20,000ft, the 17kVA alternator will generate sufficient power to drive the powered flying control units and other services necessary to maintain the aircraft in flight.

7 Functional testing of the RAT is made by passing a jet of high pressure air over the fan blades and measuring the amount of electrical power generated.

8 Ram Air Turbine installation.

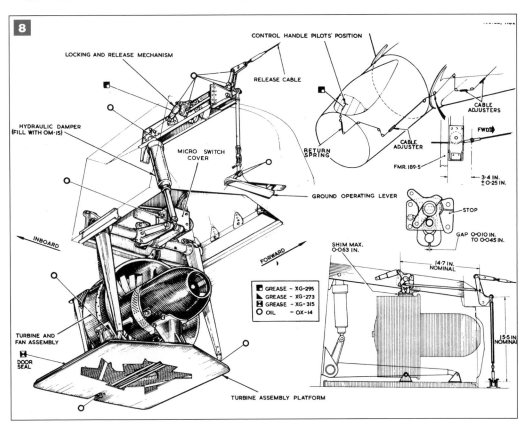

ELECTRICAL SYSTEMS

Whether it is on the ground or in the air, the Vulcan is completely dependent on the correct functioning of its electrical systems. In total some five miles of electrical wiring needed to be replaced on XH558, with much of it laid through areas in the bowels of the aircraft where it was difficult to reach.

1 'Let chaos reign!' The pilots' instrument panel pictured mid-way through its restoration. Fortunately, the RAF technical manuals contained electrical diagrams to serve as 'road maps'

2 Rex Gulliver connects up the new wiring on the pilots' instrument panel.

3 Kevin 'Taff' Stone at work in the rear of the nose wheel undercarriage bay, where he is seen pulling in the replacement wiring.

4 Ron Evans works on the emergency hydraulic power pack. This unit provides not only the hydraulic pressure necessary to open the bomb bay doors, but also to charge the brake accumulators in the event of a failure of the main system.

5 Pat Bowyer is pictured in the electrical servicing bay carrying out functional tests on the refuelling panels, which are located inside the port and starboard undercarriage bays.

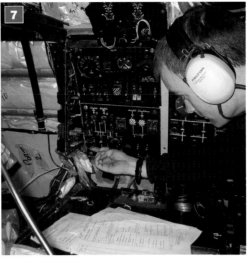

6 Lying down on the job. An electrician gets stuck into the business of laying down replacement wiring behind the AEO's console.

7 The AEO's electrical panel receives attention.

FUEL SYSTEM

The Vulcan carries its fuel in fourteen tanks, seven on each side, built into the wings and fuselage. The flow of fuel from the tanks on either side is controlled automatically by a 'proportioner'. This device ensures that the tanks give up their fuel at a rate proportional to their capacity, thereby ensuring that aircraft's centre of gravity remains constant.

1 Alan Rolf (left) and co-author Andrew Edmondson carry out a check of the fuel pressurisation control panel.

2 The underside of the wing, looking up at a fuel tank and the fuel pump.

3 Ron Evans fits the installation buttons to one of the outer wing bag fuel tanks.

4 This is a view inside a bag tank fitted in the wing. The vertical cylindrical rods are tie rods that support the bag in the airframe. At the rear are the transponders for the indicators that measure the fuel level in the tank.

WEIGHING THE AIRCRAFT

1 Weight watcher: one of the main undercarriage bogies pictured during the weighing of the aircraft. Each pair of main wheel tyres, and those of the nose wheel, sat on separate load pads. On the side of each load pad is a scale showing the weight borne by each wheel

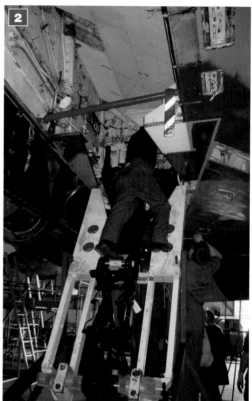

and those weights were added up to show the load on each main bogey. From these readings the total weight of the aircraft, and its centre of gravity, can be calculated.

2 The port undercarriage leg, seen from the rear. The man standing on the staging at the top centre gives an idea of the size of these units. He is working in the engine recuperator bay, where the two recuperators on that side are positioned. The purpose of these units is to force fuel up to the engines to allow them to continue to run when the aircraft is flying at zero or negative G. Such flying is not permitted in peace time, but it might have been forced on the crew in time of war.

THE FEARSOME 'BOTTOM LINE'

Keeping the Vulcan flying is not a game for the financially squeamish. For a start, hangarage costs £5,000 per month. Compared with other items of expenditure on this project, however, that is a snip.

When it comes to converting money into noise, the Vulcan knows no rival. Taking into account the full array of expenses, it costs £18,500 to have the Vulcan take off, fly to the air display venue, give its 9-minute display, then return to base. If there is a two-day event and the aircraft is required to fly to the venue, give its display, land away from base, give its display a second time on the following day and then return to base, that costs £32,500.

Problem is, your average air display cannot afford £18,500, or anything like that amount, for the Vulcan's standard display. The cost of the fuel, alone, comes to £6,500. Add a few big red-ones to cover miscellaneous overheads and pay the crews, and that establishes the absolute minimum cost of the flying display at around £12,000.

Those who enjoy haggling might like to try offering the prime sales pitch at their air show to the VTST, in return for a reduction in the cost of the display. Given a good day's merchandising and donations, VTST will end up in the black and everyone is a winner.

So much for the relatively small-change items, the sweepings off the floor in financial terms. When it is a question of really serious money, the answer is insurance. The Vulcan is covered for third party risks of up to £4,000,000, and public liability drawing rights to the equivalent of £330 million. The cost of that is a cool £235,000 per year (sucking of teeth). If the Vulcan were to be damaged beyond repair in an accident, the Lottery Fund grant of £2.74 million could suddenly re-transmute itself from pure gold back into base metal, and that amount might have to be repaid.

As we said at the beginning of this section, keeping the Vulcan flying is not a game for the financially squeamish.

EJECTION SEAT REMOVAL

Once each year it is necessary to carry out a servicing and inspection of the pilots' ejection seats. For this purpose the seats are removed from the aircraft and sent to Safety Equipment Services, based at Malmesbury in Wiltshire, a company that specialises in this work.

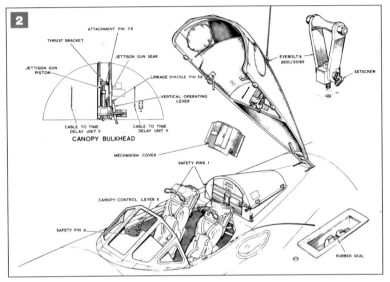

1-5 Before the ejection seats can be removed from the aircraft it is first necessary to lift off the canopy. In an emergency, an explosive ram fitted to each main gun would force the canopy upwards into the airflow, which then carries it clear. For servicing, the canopy is released by pulling one of the yellow and black-striped handles on either side of the canopy rail, which unlocks the hooks that secure the canopy in place. Then a crane fitted with a nylon strop is used to lift off the canopy and extract each ejection seat in turn.

6 An ejection seat sits on its special ground handling trolley. It will be serviced by Safety Equipment Services.

1 Looking down at a main undercarriage leg. The walking joints are on the left and the locking mechanism on the centre. *D. Petrie*

2 The port undercarriage leg seen being retracted inside its bay.

3 A close-up of the starboard undercarriage leg during the reassembly process.

4 Removal of wheel brake unit.

Close-up shots of the main undercarriage leg and the 'Maxaret' anti-skid brake unit. Each of the eight wheels on each main wheel bogie has to be inflated to a pressure of 275lbs/sq in.

BRAKE TORQUE ROD

SEALING RINGS

RETAINING WASHER

TORQUE ROD PIN RETAINING BOLT

TORQUE PIN

SEALING WASHER

SEALING WASHER

RETAINING PIN

BRAKE PIPE TRUNNION

INNER WHEEL BEARING BUSH

MAXARET ANTI-SKID UNIT

BRAKE UNIT

BLEED SCREW

5 Phil Raymond is pictured carrying out the wire locking of the 'Maxaret' anti-skid brake unit on the starboard main wheel bogie.

6 Brake units awaiting overhaul. *Jonathan Falconer*

7 The main undercarriage brake unit undergoes non-destructive testing.

8 Close-up of nose wheel main fitting, drag stay and nose wheel steering jack.

9 Nose wheel unit.

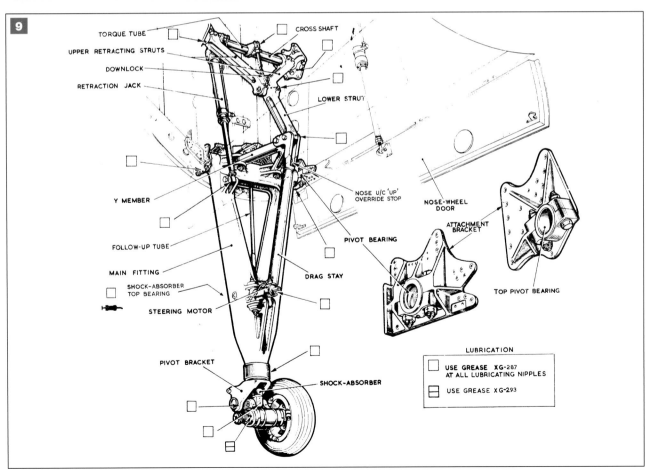

TORQUE TUBE
CROSS SHAFT
UPPER RETRACTING STRUTS
DOWNLOCK
RETRACTION JACK
LOWER STRUT
NOSE U/C 'UP' OVERRIDE STOP
NOSE-WHEEL DOOR
ATTACHMENT BRACKET
Y MEMBER
PIVOT BEARING
FOLLOW-UP TUBE
MAIN FITTING
DRAG STAY
TOP PIVOT BEARING
SHOCK-ABSORBER TOP BEARING
STEERING MOTOR
PIVOT BRACKET
SHOCK-ABSORBER

LUBRICATION
USE GREASE XG-287 AT ALL LUBRICATING NIPPLES
USE GREASE XG-293

CORROSION

1 Corrosion was found in the underside roof of the main undercarriage bay. The 'J' section beams, which were badly corroded, had to be removed by grinding in the less affected areas, or by complete replacement of the beams.

2 and 3 In order to repair an area of corrosion found in the starboard wing it was first necessary to peel back the outer skin on the top surface. Then the corroded 'J' and 'Z' section structures could be removed and replaced. Here Trevor Bailey can be seen working on an affected area inside the starboard wing.

Since the bruising battle to bring corrosion under control in 2006, the technicians have been very sensitive about this condition. As a precaution, if the aircraft is caught in a rain storm or if it has been left in the open for more than two weeks, they conduct a further deep inspection of the airframe, searching for any sign of a recurrence. So far – touch wood – there has been none.

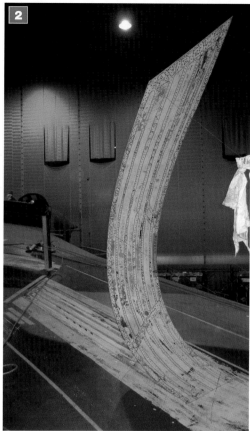

MODIFICATION 2222

When the Vulcan was designed in the early 1950s nobody could have believed that an example might still be flying more than half a century later. Metal fatigue testing had revealed the likely areas on the aircraft where failures might occur. These drove the so-called Fatigue Index (FI), which indicated how long the Vulcan could continue to fly under the stated conditions.

As XH558 progressed through its service career it used up FIs on every flight, and there began a long running programme of life extending modifications to the aircraft. From 1966 each Vulcan B2 was returned to the makers to have vulnerable components in the airframe strengthened or replaced.

British Aerospace developed – and the RAF accepted – a solution known as 'Modification 2222' to beef up the Vulcan's lower rear spar. This major operation involved disconnecting each wing from the fuselage and bolting a short stub spar made of steel onto either side of the Vulcan's lower rear spar. The modification restored the aircraft's Fatigue Index. When XH558 was sold to C. Walton Ltd it had already undergone Mod 2222 on one occasion, but if it was to have a useful display life the process needed to be repeated.

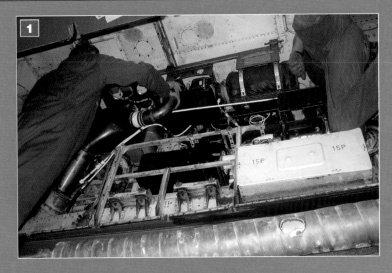

1 XH558 pictured before she received her latest Mod 2222. The previous stub spar, seen before removal, is coloured light green.
2 The steel short stub spar used in Modification 2222. The spar is about 18in long and 1in thick.
3 Colin Stirrat observes one of the steel sub spars in place in front of him, with all the holes drilled, before the insertion of the main bolts. On far right is the actuator of one of the main lifting jacks supporting the aircraft.
4 The replacement stub spar securely in place. The box marked 'SWL 5000 lb' is a trestle supporting the disconnected wing. On the far right is the bottom skin of the No 1 engine.

151

JACKING AND TRESTLING THE VULCAN

1 Fitting a jacking adaptor to prepare a jacking point before lifting.

2 and 3 Moving one of four 25-ton lifting jacks into position under the jacking point.

4 and 5 Operating one of the jacks to lift the aircraft.

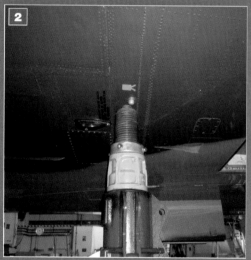

In the course of the restoration work on XH558, the engineers needed to jack up and trestle the airframe of the Vulcan eight times. That number of lifts was necessary to accommodate the large number of inspections and system functional checks required. The operation was quite different from jacking up the family Mondeo to change a wheel. In the dry condition for lifting, the Vulcan B2 weighed just a little less than 47 tons. When dealing with such a hefty but inherently fragile structure, the utmost care was necessary to avoid causing serious damage to the airframe.

The Vulcan has four main jacking points and four auxiliary points built into the airframe at eight positions in the centre fuselage. When not in use, these points have screw-in sealing caps to fair them over. Before the operation begins, the sealing caps had to be removed and replaced with the special domed screw-in jacking adaptors (see illustration).

For the lifting operation, four 25-ton hand operated hydraulic jacks were employed. When raising the aircraft, it was vitally important that all four jacks are raised evenly and simultaneously, to ensure an even distribution of the loading. The engineer in charge of the lift controlled the operation from the aircraft's crew compartment, using a levelling plate and plumb line. The levelling plate was placed on the floor at the forward end of the rear crew's compartment. The plumb line was then suspended from a special bracket near the canopy roof, immediately above the levelling plate. The plate was engraved to indicate the amount, in inches, that the corresponding jack or jacks had to be raised or lowered to achieve equilibrium. The engineer in charge of the operation called out the order to raise or lower the jacks, and his team moved them one inch at a time. After each such move, the engineer in charge checked the movement of the plumb line over the levelling plate, and ordered any necessary corrections. Typically, such a simple lifting operation might take about an hour.

The height to which the aircraft was raised depended on the type of work to be carried out. For example, when preparing for an undercarriage retraction test, it was important to have at least 6½in of clearance beneath the trailing bogie of each of the main undercarriage legs. That distance was necessary to accommodate the trail angle of the wheel bogies, as they moved through their respective arcs of retraction.

Other, more complex, lifting operations took longer. If the aircraft had to be set up in the flight rigging position, the operation might take over three hours and involve the use of a clinometer (a rather smart type of protractor) and special rigging boards.

An even more involved lift was necessary if the aircraft was to be raised to replicate the in-flight stresses in the zero G condition. In that case the aircraft was jacked to the same height as for undercarriage retraction checks. Then the wing and the nose trestles were placed in position, and the wing jacks raised by a further 2½in. That stressed the nose to a deflection of about half an inch, and allowed the engineers to remove panels, screws, rivets and bolts from the airframe. Also, importantly, the aircraft needed to be in that position when these items were replaced.

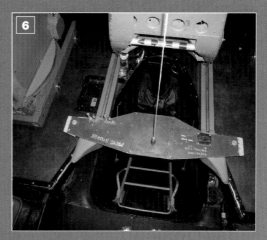

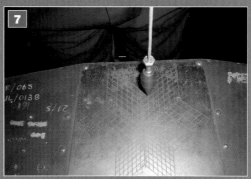

6 This photograph shows the levelling plate, seen from above looking down through the entrance door. To the left and to the right are the circular bases of the AEO's and the navigator radar's seats. The plumb bob hanging from its attachment point in the ceiling measures the exact vertical on the plate.

7 Close up of the plumb bob over the levelling plate. The lines etched on the plate showed how accurately the aircraft was positioned on its jacks, with its weight spread evenly between all four jacks. In this case the aircraft was a little to the left of the centre line, with its nose slightly up, the right wing slightly low and the nose higher than the main wheels.

8 Once the aircraft was raised in the correct position, trestles are moved into place to support other parts of the aircraft.

9 Hoisting and securing the air conditioning unit into position in the forward port side of the nose wheel undercarriage bay. This unit provides pressurised, warmed or cooled air for the crew compartment as selected.

Avro Vulcan Timeline

December 1946

Requirement specification for new heavy bomber B35/46 issued.

December 1946

British government takes the decision to develop and build a nuclear weapon.

March 1947

Avro Type 698 sketched out as a pure flying wing bomber.

27 November 1947

Avro's design tender to B35/46 accepted.

June 1948

Construction of two Avro Type 698 prototypes ordered.

September 1948

Detailed design of the Avro Type 698 completed.

4 September 1948

First flight of Avro 707 VX284, a one-third scale Type 698 bomber. Aircraft crashed less than a month later.

6 September 1950

First flight of Avro 707B XW790.

February 1951

First flight of Avro 707B with modified air intakes.

June 1951

First flight of Avro 707A WD280.

July 1952

First Production order for Avro Type 698s.

6 August 1952

First British atomic weapon test, at Monte Bello Island in the Pacific.

30 August 1952

First flight of Avro 698, VX770, powered by four RR Avon engines.

October 1952

Avro 698 officially named the Vulcan.

3 September 1953

First flight of second Vulcan prototype, VX777.

4 February 1955

First flight of first production Vulcan XA889.

5 October 1955

First flight of the second Vulcan prototype, with the kinked leading edge of the wing.

20 July 1956

First Vulcan B1 delivered to RAF Bomber Command, 230 OCU at Waddington.

15 May 1957

Valiant of 49 Squadron made the first live test drop of a British thermonuclear weapon near Maldon Island in the South Pacific.

11 July 1957

Delivery of the first Vulcan B1 to an operational unit, 83 Squadron at Waddington.

31 August 1957

Second prototype Vulcan flies with the enlarged B2 wing.

19 August 1958

First flight of the Vulcan B2.

30 April 1959

Last Vulcan B1 delivered, of 25 built.

1 July 1960

Delivery of the first Vulcan B2 to OCU at Waddington.

October 1960

Programme commences to convert all Vulcan B1 aircraft to B1A standard, by the addition of ECM equipment in the tail cone and a bleed air turbine to produce the necessary power. This programme continued until May 1963.

December 1960

First delivery of Vulcan B2 to an operational RAF unit, 83 Squadron at Scampton.

21 September 1961

Vulcan tested with wings modified to carry two shapes of the Skybolt air launched ballistic missile, a weapon that was earmarked for the Vulcan.

December 1962

The US government abandoned the development of the Skybolt long range stand-off missile, which was to have replaced the Blue Steel.

February 1963

First squadron operational with the Blue Steel stand-off missile, 617 Squadron at Scampton.

Spring 1964

RAF V-force bombers switched to low level attack profiles.

4 January 1965

Last Vulcan B2 delivered.

30 June 1969

The nuclear-powered Polaris submarine HMS *Resolution* set sail on her first war patrol. At the end of the month the Royal Navy took over responsibility for the United Kingdom Deterrent Force.

December 1970

Blue Steel missile withdrawn from RAF service, all remaining Vulcan B2As being converted to the free-fall bombing role.

June 1981

Phased withdrawal of the Vulcan force commences.

April-May 1982

Under operation 'Black Buck', Vulcans flew five attacks against targets around Port Stanley in the Falkland Islands.

30 June 1983

First of six Vulcan B2K tanker conversions delivered to 50 Squadron.

31 December 1982

Last Vulcan B2 Squadron disbanded.

31 March 1984

Vulcan B2K tanker withdrawn from service.

23 March 1993

Last official Vulcan flight, to deliver XH558 to Bruntingthorpe airfield, Leicestershire, to C. Walton Ltd, its new civilian owner.

September 1999

The launch of a campaign to return Vulcan XH558 to flight.

22 June 2004

The Heritage Lottery Fund awards £2.4m towards the cost of the restoration of Vulcan XH558.

18 October 2007

XH558 made its first flight after restoration.

3 July 2008

XH558 received its official Permit to Fly from the British Civil Aviation Authority. That afternoon it flew to RAF Waddington to demonstrate its display routine, and received its Display Authorisation to allow it to display before the public.

2009 Season

A successful display season. Of 37 displays or fly-bys booked, 3 were cancelled for technical reasons and two fell foul of bad weather. But the other 32 events went ahead as planned.

September 2009

The aircraft landed at RAF Lyneham and went into the hangar there for winter servicing.

February 2010

The receipt of a bequest for £458,000 from an anonymous donor placed VTTS on a firm footing for the 2010 display season.

Surviving Vulcans

At the time of writing, nineteen complete Vulcans, all B2s, remain in existence. Of these, fifteen are in Great Britain, three are in the USA and one is in Canada.

GREAT BRITAIN
XH558 Watch this space   *Flight-worthy*
XJ823 Carlisle Airport, Cumbria
XJ824 Imperial War Museum, Duxford
XL318 RAF Museum Hendon, London
XL319 North East Aircraft Museum, Sunderland
XL360 Midland Air Museum, Coventry, Warwickshire
XL426 Southend Airport, Essex   *Engine runs only*
XM575 East Midlands Airport, Castle Donington, Leicestershire
XM594 Newark Air Museum, Nottinghamshire
XM597 Museum of Flight, East Fortune, East Lothian
XM598 Aerospace Museum, Cosford, Shropshire
XM603 Woodford, Greater Manchester
XM607 RAF Waddington, Lincolnshire
XM612 Aviation Museum, Norwich Airport, Norfolk
XM655 Wellesbourne Airport, Warwickshire   *Engine runs only*

OVERSEAS
XL361 Goose Bay, Labrador, Canada
XM573 Strategic Air Command Museum, Ashland, Nebraska, USA
XM605 US Air Force Museum, Castle Air Force Base, California, USA
XM606 Barksdale Air Force Base, Louisiana, USA

With acknowledgements to Guy Bartlett and website http://studysupport. info/vulcanbomber

RIGHT XH558's ground crew with Crew Chief Kevin 'Taff' Stone (centre).
Vulcan to the Sky Trust

Appendix C
Glossary of Terms

AEO	Air Electronics Officer.
AAPP	Airborne Auxiliary Power Plant. Small turbojet engine fitted under the starboard wing of the Vulcan that provided electrical power and compressed air for starting the main engines.
Blue Diver	Metric wavelength radar jamming system.
Blue Saga	Radar warning receiver.
Blue Steel	Stand-off nuclear missile carried by some Vulcan B2s.
Carcinotron	Power source for the Red Shrimp noise jammer. The centre frequency of the jammer and the band width of the jamming could be adjusted by altering the voltages at the electrodes.
Chaff	Metal foil or metalised fibreglass dropped to confuse enemy radars.
CSDU	Constant speed drive unit, fitted to each of the Vulcan B2's alternators to allow outputs to be synchronised.
Doppler	Navigational equipment using radar to measure the aircraft's ground speed and drift.
ECM	Electronic countermeasures.
Fan Song	NATO codename for Soviet missile guidance radar built in large numbers and widely deployed.
GEE	Hyperbolic radar navigational system.
Green Palm	VHF communications jammer.
Green Satin	See Doppler.
H2S	Bombing radar fitted to all V-bomber aircraft.
MFS	Military Flight System.
NBS	Navigation Bombing System. Main attack system fitted to V-bombers, combining the H2S with the bombing computers.
QRA	Quick Reaction Alert. Crews and aircraft in a combat ready state, ready to take-off at short notice to attack previously designated targets.
RAT	Ram Air Turbine. Small turbine mounted under the port wing, which could be lowered into the airflow to produce electrical power in an emergency.
Red Shrimp	Carcinatron noise jammer fitted to the Vulcan.
Rope	Reels of metal foil, released to confuse enemy long wavelength radars.
Red Steer	Tail warning radar fitted to the Vulcan.
Skybolt	Long range (approximately 1,000 miles) stand-off missile built by the Douglas Company, intended to replace Blue Steel in the RAF. During tests Skybolt proved disappointing and the US government cancelled the project.
TACAN	Tactical Navigation System, which measured the aircrafts' range and bearing from ground beacons.
TFR	Terrain Following Radar.
TVOC	The Vulcan Operating Company. Small group formed in 1997 to examine the possibility of restoring XH558 to flight.
VCCP	Vapour Cycle Cooling Pack, necessary to allow the high powered jamming transmitters to run without building up excessive heat which would burn them out.
VTST	Vulcan to the Sky Trust. A registered charitable trust, formed to allow the Vulcan restoration team to bid for a grant from the Heritage Lottery Fund.

157
GLOSSARY OF TERMS

Index

AAPP (Auxiliary Airborne Power Plant)
16, 68, 75-6, 80, 88, 94, 112-3, 125,
131, 142
Aberporth range 18
Adams, Ron 145
AEO's station 106, 111-3, 145
AERE Aldermaston 29
Air brakes 11, 28, 70, 77, 92-3, 119-20
Air conditioning unit 153
Airframe 54-63, 116
Air intakes 10-1, 16, 58, 68, 90, 120,
141
Air Ministry 8-10, 98
Operational Requirement OR229 8-9
Requirement B.35/46 10
Air systems 116, 120
Alert standby 88
Argentine Air Force 49
Comodoro Rivadavia airfield 49
Gruppo 8 49
Rio Gallegos airfield 49
Armstrong Whitworth 8
Astro-navigation 103
Autopilot 95
Avro 8, 18, 94
Lancaster 7, 9, 27, 131
Tudor 10
698 Vulcan 9-10
B1 9, 14, 16-8, 24, 68, 79-80, 101
B1A 17, 24, 91, 111
B2 15-6, 24, 27, 35, 51, 61, 68-9,
74, 79-80, 88, 94-5, 102, 111-2
B2 (MRR) 32
B2A 20
B (K) 2 tanker 32-5
prototypes 7-8, 12-14, 16
707 10-13; 707A 11-2; 707B 11
A.V. Roe Co. 125

BAe Systems – see also British
Aerospace 125-7
Baldwin, Wg Cdr Simon 38
Barrel rolls 13
Battle of Britain Memorial Flight 27,
35, 131
Beagle Aerospace 129, 136
Beetham, Air Chief Marshal Sir
Michael 44
Beushaw, Peter 125-6
B.F. Goodrich 126

Biglands, Flt Lt Steve 41-2
Blackburn Buccaneer 31, 43, 125
Blackman, Tony 16, 55, 79-80, 94
Boeing B-52 20
Bomb-aiming system 44, 54, 99,
101-2, 130
Bomb bay 19, 30, 56-8, 71-2, 90, 100
doors 76-7, 120, 124, 144
switches 76
Bomber Command Navigation
Competition 103
Bombs – see also Nuclear weapons
1,000lb high explosive 14, 38, 43,
49, 61, 102
Boston, Lincolnshire and USA 24
Boulton Paul 126
Bowyer, Pat 144
Boyle, John 140
Bracknell meteorological
office 29
Brake parachute 77, 93, 95, 120-1,
124
Bristol Aero Engine Co. 115
British Aerospace – see also BAe
Systems 151
Hawk 132
Bruntingthorpe 49, 88, 124-8, 130,
135, 137
'Big Thunder' air display 124-5

Certificate of Airworthiness 14
Chadwick, Roy 9-10
Chaff and Rope dispensers 106,
109-11
Chater, Ann and Tony 44
CIA 23
Cisco Systems 125
Civil Aviation Authority (CAA) 125-8
Display Authorisation 131
Permit to Fly 128, 131
Clark, Nick 138, 143
Clothing 18, 22
Cockpit/flight deck/instrument panel
80-7, 95, 116, 120, 144, 147
Cockpit canopy 11, 55-6, 83,
119-120, 125
Cold War 25, 128
Communications suite 112
Concorde 64
Control column 70, 81, 93, 116

Cooper, Mick 49
Crashes and accidents 11, 13-4,
24-5, 69
Cruising altitude 89
C. Walton Ltd 124-8, 151

Davies, Stuart 10
Defensive systems 61
de Havilland Sea Vixen 29
De-icing systems 61, 63
Deliveries to RAF 14, 17, 79, 95
Demonstration and display flights 14-6,
24, 29, 81, 121, 123, 131-3, 146
Dowty (Messier-Dowty) 126
Dunlop 126

ECM (electronic counter measures) –
see also Radar and radio systems
16-7, 23, 27, 35, 51, 62, 68, 108,
110-113, 130
ALQ-101 jamming pod 43
Blue Diver noise jammers 62, 106,
108, 111
cooling system 63, 105, 110
Green Palm VHF jammer 62-3,
106, 108
Red Shrimp noise jammer 106, 108,
110-1
noise jammers 16, 43
Eden, Sir Anthony 13
Edmondson, Andrew 124-8, 130, 132,
145
Electrical systems 12, 16-7, 68-9, 75,
80, 94-5, 112, 142-5
alternators 94, 113, 120, 140, 142-3
failure/emergency power 80, 113,
142-3
Elliott Bros 102
Ems, Rob 138
Engine controls 16
Engine failures 16, 90
Engine installation and removal 139-
141
Engine starting 67, 88, 94, 117, 120,
142
high energy ignition units 129
Palouste rig 116, 119-120
rapid starting 27, 67, 88, 94,
116, 120
relighting 16-7, 90, 95

Engines
  Armstrong Siddeley Sapphire 12
  Bristol BE 10 Olympus 12-4, 51,
    63, 125
    101 14, 65; 102 14; 103 65;
      104 14, 17
  Rolls-Royce Avon 12
  Rolls-Royce Derwent 10
  Rolls-Royce (ex-Bristol)
    Olympus 63-9
    200 Series 15-6, 64; 201 61,
      63-5, 94
    301 27, 65, 68
    593 64
English Electric 8
  Canberra 31, 97-9, 105, 115
  Lightning T5 90
Escape and survival systems 22-3, 25
  ejection seats 25, 55, 80, 87, 118-
    20, 147
  escape chutes 25, 80
Evans, Ron 137, 144
Evans, Sam 143

Falk, Roly 11-3
Falkland Conflict 32, 37-45, 48-9, 102
  Task Force 49
Farnborough Air Show 1952 7-8, 12;
    1953 13; 1958 16; 2008 123
Fatigue life 24-5, 151
Fisher, David 137-8
Flight magazine 14
Flight Reference Cards (Pilots' Notes)
  80, 88
Flying controls systems 80-1, 94, 113,
  116, 119, 136-8, 142
Flying on two engines 90
Fuel system 71-2, 81, 94-5, 126, 145
  gauges 81, 85, 94
  pumps 66, 69, 145
  refuelling – see also In-flight 116-7,
    144
  tanks 9, 12, 30, 71-2, 81, 95,
    116, 145
Fuselage 54-9
  front pressure bulkhead 55, 71
Fylingdales radar site 91, 103

Giant Voice exercise 103
Gloster Meteor 19
Graham, Flt Lt Gordon 40
Gulliver, Rex 144

Handley Page 8
  HP 80 Victor 9-10, 12-3, 24, 111,
  125
  B.2 7, 111
  tanker 32, 38-42, 44-6, 49

Handling 10, 79-80
  high speed 11
  low speed 11-2
Hands, Steve 141
Hawker Hunter 125
Hawker Siddeley
  Nimrod 31
  Sea Harrier 49
Hayr, Air Vice-Marshal Kenneth 44
Hayward, Sir Jack 129
Heritage Lottery Fund 127-8, 146
High altitude flying 22-3, 90-2, 102,
  106, 110-2, 142
Hydraulic systems 12, 69, 75-6, 88,
  144

Ilyushin 28 98
In-flight refuelling (tanking) 14-5, 32,
  34-5, 38-42, 44-7, 49, 51, 72
  refuelling probe 30, 54

Jacking and trestling 151-3
Jefford, 'Jeff' 97, 106
Jet pipes 59, 66, 94-5, 116, 120, 125,
  141

Kent, HRH Duke of 132
Kirby, Ron 144
Knight, Sir Michael 127

Landing (touchdown) 28, 92-3, 95
Landing gear (undercarriage) 12, 25,
  73-5, 77, 94, 116, 119, 126, 146,
  148-9
  bogies 73, 146, 149
  brakes 120, 126, 148-9
  door latch 74
  main wheel units 73, 146, 148-9, 153
  nose wheel unit 11, 25, 56, 75,
    146, 149
  nose wheel steering 88, 94
  retraction 88-9, 153
  tyres 120
  undercarriage bays 74-5, 119,
    144, 150, 153
Lockheed
  F-117 113
  U-2 23
London-Heathrow Airport 14
Low altitude flying 18, 23-5, 27, 31, 91,
  102, 111-2, 142
Lucas 126

Mach trimmer 13, 89, 95
Maiden flights 12-3, 17, 130-2
Mail on Sunday, The 133
Manoeuvrability 13
Mans, Keith 125

Marshall Aerospace 126, 129
Masefield, Barry 49
McDonnell Phantom 34, 124
Medium altitude flying 25, 102
Military Flight System (MFS) 91
Ministry of Defence 44, 124
Mirage III 49
Missiles: air-to-air 49, 112
Missiles: air-to-surface
  Blue Steel 18-20, 31, 51, 61, 89, 98,
    100, 102-3
  Douglas Skybolt 20, 24, 79
Missiles: anti-radar
  Shrike 48-9
Missiles: surface-to-air 110, 112
  S-75 (NATO SA-2) 23, 108

NATO 31
Navigation lights 62
Navigator's station and system 98-102,
  111
Northrop Grumman B-2 stealth bomber
  113
Nuclear/thermonuclear weapons 14
  Blue Danube 14, 101
  US Mk 5 megaton (H) 14, 101
  Violet Club 14, 18, 101
  Yellow Sun 14-5, 20, 61, 102, 106
  W59 20
  WE177 14, 102

Oil systems 120
Operation 'Aroma' 29
Operation 'Black Buck' 38-40, 43,
  48-9, 91
Operation 'Corporate' 37

Paint schemes 7, 14, 24, 106
Panavia Tornado 32, 124
Pick, Earl 125
Pitch damping 10, 13, 89, 95
Pleming, Dr Robert 125, 127, 132-3
Pneumatic system 77
Polaris submarine-launched missile 20,
  27, 112
Porter, Sqn Ldr John 33
Port Stanley 38-9, 42-4
  airfield bombing 38, 42-5, 49
Post-flight inspection 120-2
Powered flying controls (PFCs) 60,
  69-70, 126, 136-7, 143
  artificial feel systems 70, 88-9, 138
Powers, Gary 23
Pre-flight inspection 116-120
  crew chief checks 118-9
Price, Alfred 29, 105-6
Prior, Flt Lt Hugh 40, 43-4
Pucara 44

Quick Reaction Alert (QRA) 14

Radar and radio systems – see also
  ECM 27, 68, 100-1, 106-8
  Blue Saga warning system 27,
    106, 108
  Doppler system 101-3
  Green Satin 102-3
  forward-looking narrow beam 91
  H2S bombing 54, 62, 130
  IFF system 106
  Navigator 55, 100-3
radomes 30, 55
Red Steer tail warning 27, 106, 109,
  112
  TACAN 102-103
  terrain following radar (TFR) 27,
    30, 91
Radar signature 113
Royal Aircraft Establishment (RAE),
  Farnborough 9
RAF air bases
  Akrotiri 30-1, 115
  Boscombe Down (A&AEE) 9, 12,
    14, 80
  Brize Norton 133
  Coningsby 105
  Cottesmore 131
  Finningley 17, 25, 105
  Lyneham 133
  Scampton 7, 14, 18-9, 29, 31, 51,
    74, 97, 115, 117, 121
  Waddington 14, 17, 27-8, 31, 38,
    79, 90, 95, 115, 124, 131
RAF Historical Society 97
RAF Museum, Cosford 20
RAF commands, squadron and units
  Bomber Command 27
  Bomber Command Development
    Unit 17
  Fighter Command 27
  Germany 34
  Maintenance Unit, Stafford 125
  Near East Bomber Wing 30-1
  Scampton Wing 18-9, 105
  Strike Command 27
  230 OCU 14, 17, 27-8, 32, 79, 95
  9 Squadron 27, 31, 105
  12 Squadron 27
  19 Squadron 34
  27 Squadron 18, 27, 29, 31-3, 97
  35 Squadron 27, 31-2
  44 Squadron 14, 27, 32, 103
  50 Squadron 14, 27, 32, 72, 90, 97
  83 Squadron 14, 18, 20, 31, 97,
    117, 121

101 Squadron 14, 27, 32, 90
617 Squadron 7, 14-5, 18, 20, 27,
  31-2, 51, 81, 115
RAT (Ram Air Turbine) 16, 80, 95, 113,
  142-3
Raymond, Phil 149
Regan, Tony 115-6
Reconnaissance role 31-2
Red Arrows 132
Red Flag exercise 81, 103
Reeve, John 49
Restoration of XH558 123-51
  corrosion 128, 130, 136, 150
  costs 146
  design copyrights 126
  first flights 130-2
Roberts, Neil 150
Rocket motors
  Aerojet 20
  de Havilland (later Bristol Siddeley)
  Stentor 18-9
Rolf, Alan 145
Royal Navy 27, 49, 112
Russell, Flt Lt Dick 42, 49

Safety Equipment Services 147
'Save the Vulcan' petition 124
Seats – see also Escape and survival
  systems 80, 99
Short Brothers 8
  SA-4 Sperrin 8-11
Smith, Terry 124
'Sound Barrier' (compressibility) 8
Soviet Air Force/Air Defence 111-2
Speeds 89, 92, 94, 131
Stability 11, 13
  artificial aids 11, 13-4
Stalling behaviour 10
Stirrat, Colin 151
Supermarine Spitfire PR19 35

Tail unit 54
  fairing 17
  fin and rudder 10, 13, 62, 70, 81,
    92, 112, 129, 136, 138
Take-offs 11, 27, 88
  Blue Steel 89
  rotation 88, 94
  scramble 27, 112
Taylor, Flg Off Peter 40
Taxiing 88
Teddington Seals 126
Test flights 13, 79, 94-5, 131
Thatcher, Lady Margaret 49
Thomas, David 125
Thorpe, David 124-5

Todd, Sqn Ldr Martin 41
Transport Trust award 132
Trappers' sortie 33
TRW 126
Tupolev 16 98
Tuxford, Sqn Ldr Bob 39, 41-2, 49
TVOC (The Vulcan Operating Co.)
  125-7, 129

Undercarriage – see Landing
  gear 144
US Air Force 20, 103, 110
  Barksdale AFB, Louisiana 103
  Nellis AFB, Nevada 81
  Offutt AFB, Nebraska 29

Vickers
  VC10 29
    K2 tanker 72
  660 Valiant 9-12, 24-5, 111
    tanker 15
Vinales, Jim 49
Vulcan Crew Chief Register 115
Vulcan Display Flight 123
Vulcan Technical Library 127
Vulcan Test Pilot book 25
Vulcan to the Sky Trust (VTST)
  127-130, 133, 146

Walton, David 124-125
Weight and weighing 90, 92, 146,
  152
West, Sqn Ldr Peter 29, 31, 33
Wideawake airfield, Ascension Island
  38-40, 44-5, 49
Wings (mainplanes) 15, 54, 60-2, 145
  ailerons 16, 70
  crescent-shaped 9
  delta 9, 11, 54, 60-1
  drag and buffeting 11, 13
  elevators 10-1, 16, 69, 138
  elevons 16, 60, 69-70, 80-1, 92, 94,
    129, 136-7
  kinked leading edge 61
  leading edge modifications 11,
    13-4
  Modification 2222 151
  redesigned, larger 15-6, 24
  vortex generators 11
Withers, Flt Lt Martin 39-46, 48-9, 91
Woodford works 13, 32, 79
Wright, Flt Lt Bob 40, 43-5

Yaw dampers 90

Zero G condition 153